KS2 ENGLISH IS EASY

(ENGLISH COMPREHENSION)

www.How2Become.com

As part of this product you have also received FREE access to online tests that will help you to pass Key Stage 2 ENGLISH COMPREHENSION.

To gain access, simply go to:

www.PsychometricTestsOnline.co.uk

Get more products for passing any test at:

www.How2Become.com

Orders: Please contact How2Become Ltd, Suite 14, 50 Churchill Square Business Centre, Kings Hill, Kent ME19 4YU.

You can order through Amazon.co.uk under ISBN 9781910602867, via the website www.How2Become.com or through Gardners.com.

ISBN: 9781910602867

First published in 2016 by How2Become Ltd.

Typeset for How2Become Ltd by Anton Pshinka.

Disclaimer

CONTENTS

GUIDANCE FOR PARENTS

Whilst the SATs are a daunting, disliked and often maligned concept, they remain an essential part of a child's education. Children should be provided with the best tools and guidance to enhance their intellectual ability and improve their performance.

The purpose of this publication is to guide you through the Key Stage 2 English test (Reading and Comprehension). It will allow you to familiarise yourself with all of the important information, advice and tips that your child will need in order to achieve exam success.

The NEW SATs

From the summer of 2016, the SATs will undergo considerable changes, as dictated by the new national curriculum.

The purpose of the new and revised SATs is to ensure these tests remain rigorous, and therefore prove to be of a much higher standard compared to previous years.

With the new national curriculum comes a new marking scheme. Whilst we cannot provide details of exactly what this marking scheme consists of, we know that your child's tests will be marked externally. The scores of these tests will be used to monitor the progress of each school's performance, which is done via Ofsted reports and League tables.

Ultimately, your child's scores in their SATs will be used in conjunction with classroom assessments to provide a general overview of their attainment and progression during that academic year.

For more information on the new national curriculum, please visit the Department for Education section on the Government's website.

When Do The New SATs Come Into Place?

The new national curriculum for Key Stage 2 SATs will be assessed for the first time in May 2016.

What Do The New SATs Cover?

The national curriculum for Key Stage 2 SATs will consist of the following:

- English Reading (Comprehension);
- English Grammar (Grammar, Punctuation and Spelling);
- Maths (Arithmetic and Reasoning);
- Science (Biology, Chemistry and Physics)*.

*(*Please note that not all children completing the SATs will sit a Science SAT. A selection of schools will be required to take part in a science sampling every other year.)*

For more revision guides including KS2 English Grammar, Punctuation and Spelling, and English Practice Papers, please visit www.amazon.co.uk and type the book title into Search.

Top Tips For Parents

In order for your child to score highly in their SATs, you need to ensure that they have everything they need to achieve high marks!

It is important that you and your child are fully aware of what the SATs consist of. The more familiar you are with what to expect, the better their chances will be when they sit down to take the tests.

Below is a list of GOLDEN NUGGETS that will help you AND your child to prepare for the Key Stage 2 SATs.

• Golden Nugget 1 – Revision timetables

When it comes to exams, preparation is key. That is why you need to sit down with your child and come up with an efficient and well-structured revision timetable.

It is important that you work with your child to assess their academic strengths and weaknesses, in order to carry out these revision sessions successfully.

TIP *– Focus on their weaker areas first!*

TIP *– Create a weekly revision timetable to work through different subject areas.*

TIP *– Spend time revising with your child. Your child will benefit from your help and this is a great way for you to monitor their progress.*

• Golden Nugget 2 – Understanding the best way your child learns

There are many different ways to revise when it comes to exams, and it all comes down to picking the way that your child will find most useful.

Below is a list of the common learning styles that you may want to try with your child:

- **Visual** – the use of pictures and images to remember information;
- **Aural** – the use of sound and music to remember information;
- **Verbal** – the use of words, in both speech and writing, to understand information;
- **Social** – working together in groups;
- **Solitary** – working and studying alone.

Popular revision techniques include: *mind mapping, flash cards, making notes, drawing flow charts,* and *diagrams*. You could instruct your child on how to turn diagrams and pictures into words, and words into diagrams. Try as many different methods as possible to see which style your child learns from the most.

***TIP** – Work out what kind of learner your child is. What method will they benefit from the most?*

***TIP** – Try a couple of different learning aids and see if you notice a change in your child's ability to understand what is being taught.*

• Golden Nugget 3 – Break times

Allow your child plenty of breaks when revising.

It's really important not to overwork your child, particularly for tests such as the SATs, which are not marked on a pass or fail basis.

***TIP** – Practising for 10 to 15 minutes per day will improve your child's reading ability.*

• Golden Nugget 4 – Practice, practice and more practice!

Purchase past practice papers. Although the curriculum will have changed for 2016, practice papers are still a fantastic way for you to gain an idea of how your child is likely to be tested.

- ## Golden Nugget 5 – Variety is key!

Make sure that your child reads a VARIETY of different literary texts. Broadening their understanding of different genres, styles and formats will help them prepare effectively for reading comprehension.

TIP *– Take your child to a library and let them discover different types of books. This will greatly increase their understanding of different literary styles.*

- ## Golden Nugget 6 – Encourage your child to discuss their work

When your child is undergoing practice questions, ask your child to talk about what they have just read. Did they understand it? Did they know what all the words meant?

TIP *– Sit down with your child and ask them questions about what they have just read. Have them read a page and then test their knowledge by creating questions about the text. Have they understood everything?*

- ## Golden Nugget 7 – Stay positive!

The most important piece of preparation advice we can give you is to make sure that your child is positive and relaxed about these tests.

Don't let the SATs worry you, and certainly don't let them worry your child.

TIP *– Make sure the home environment is as comfortable and relaxed as possible for your child.*

• Golden Nugget 8 – Answer the easier questions first

A good tip to teach your child is to answer all the questions they find easiest first. That way, they can swiftly work through the questions before attempting the questions they struggle with.

TIP *– Get your child to undergo a practice paper. Tell them to fill in the answers that they find the easiest first. That way, you can spend time helping your child with the questions they find more difficult.*

Spend some time working through the questions they find difficult and make sure that they know how to work out the answer.

• Golden Nugget 9 – Make sure they refer back to the text

One of the biggest mistakes a child can make in their Reading Comprehension SAT, is that they don't refer back to the text. All of the answers can be found in the text, therefore they should support their answers with information taken from the passage, as opposed to relying on their memory.

• Golden Nugget 10 – Understanding key terms

The next section is a glossary containing all the KEY TERMS that your child should familiarise themselves with.

Sit down with your child and learn as many of these KEY TERMS as you can.

TIP *– Why not make your child's learning fun? Write down all of the key terms and cut them out individually. Do the same for the definitions.*

Get your child to try and match the KEY TERM with its definition. Keep playing this game until they get them all right!

LEARN YOUR KEY TERMS (A to Z)

ADJECTIVE	A 'describing' word. A word used to describe what something *looks, feels, smells* or *tastes* like. Adjectives also tell us how someone is feeling.
ADVERB	Adverbs are words that describe a verb. These words tend to tell us *how* something is being done, or given more information on *what* is being done.
ALLITERATION	The repetition of the same sound or letter used at the beginning of adjacent or closely connected words.
ANTONYM	An antonym refers to a word which has the **opposite** meaning to another.
APOSTROPHE (')	An apostrophe is a punctuation mark used to (1) indicate belonging or (2) to show letters have been omitted, which forms a contraction. *(See contractions.)*
AUTHOR	The writer or creator of that particular literary text.
CHARACTERISATION	The way in which an actor (in a play) acts out their role. Bringing a character to life.
CHARACTERS	The people that appear in a literary text.
CLAUSE	A clause is a part of a sentence that contains a verb and a subject.
COLON (:)	A punctuation mark used to (1) join sentences, (2) introduce lists, (3) introduce a quotation or (4) introduce explanations.
COMMA (,)	A punctuation mark used to (1) indicate a pause between parts of sentences or (2) to separate items into a list format.
CONJUNCTION	A conjunction is a word that joins phrases or words together.
CONTEXT	Identifying meaning of the literary text, based on the use of words, the time it was written, circumstances and situation.
CONTRACTION	Contractions are 'shorthand' ways of writing words. It is one word usually made up of two words. *For example, the word 'don't' is made up of the words 'do' and 'not'.*

DASH **(–)**	A dash is used to separate information. It is stronger than a comma, but not as formal as a colon. Not to be confused with a hyphen (a dash line is longer).
DETERMINER	A determiner is a word that goes before a noun in order to clarify it.
DIALOGUE	Spoken speech (a conversation) between two or more people.
ELLIPSIS **(...)**	An ellipsis is a set of three dots (full stops) which can (1) add suspense, (2) leave a sentence hanging or (3) show interruptions or missing words.
EVIDENCE	A way of supporting your answers by using ACTUAL proof from the passage.
EXCLAMATION MARK **(!)**	An exclamation mark is used to show a command or something that is forceful or surprising.
FACT	True pieces of information.
FICTION	A literary style in the form of prose (novels). These events and people are imaginary – it is invented / not from real life.
FIGURATIVE LANGUAGE	A figure of speech that goes beyond the literal meaning. For example, *metaphors, similes, hyperbole, personification*.
FULL STOP **(.)**	A full stop should be used to end a sentence.
HOMONYMS	These are words that *sound* and are *spelled* the same, but have different meanings.
HOMOPHONES	These are words that *sound* the same but are spelt differently, and have different meanings.
HYPERBOLE	Exaggeration of ideas, not meant to be taken literally, but used as a way to emphasise something.
INFERENCES	A conclusion based on evidence and reasoning.
INVERTED COMMAS **(“ ”)**	Inverted commas are used to show direct speech or quotation. These can either be single (‘) or double (“). Inverted commas can also be used to draw attention to something unusual, ironic or arguably incorrect.

LANGUAGE	The way in which something is written or communicated.
LEGENDS	An old form of literature. A combination of myth and historical fact to describe a hero or figure.
METAPHORS	Non-literal words or phrases used to make comparisons between people, objects, places or animals.
MODERN LITERATURE	Texts written or based in the contemporary period.
MYTHS	Ancient stories about how the world was created, the natural world and the spiritual truths. They also refer to ideas or beliefs that are untrue.
NON-FICTION	Writing that is based on true / real-life events or facts. It provides the reader with real and factual information.
NOUN	A word that names something.
OPINIONS	Statements that might not be true. They are based on personal beliefs and personal thoughts.
PARAGRAPHS	A way of breaking up text, in order for the passage to flow better. Each paragraph usually deals with a different theme or idea. Indicated by a new or indented line.
PERSONIFICATION	Giving human or personal characteristics to inanimate objects.
PLAYS	A type of literary style which involves dialogue between characters. Often intended for theatrical productions.
PLURAL	More than one of something. Opposite to 'singular'.
POETRY	A style of literary work which is based on feelings and ideas, using styles, rhythms, verses and composition.
PREDICTIONS	A way of guessing or forecasting what *could* or *might* happen after or in the future.
PREFIX	A prefix is added to the beginning of a word to make a new word.

PREPOSITION	A preposition tells us where something is or how they are related.
PRESENTATION	The way something is portrayed to its readers / audience.
PRONOUN	A word that replaces the noun.
PROSE	A form of ordinary language which has no formal rhythmic structure. A natural flow of written or verbal speech.
QUESTION MARK (?)	A question mark is used to show a question.
REPETITION	The act of repeating something that has already been said or written. Used for effect to emphasise a point.
RHYTHM	A strong pattern of a beat that you can hear in words.
SEMI-COLON (;)	A semi-colon is used to separate longer sentences but still reads as one complete sentence, or to link two closely related sentences.
SHAKESPEARE	An English poet and playwright who wrote important sonnets and plays.
STRUCTURE	The way a literary text is laid out. The structure of a text will depend on what *type* of text it is.
SUFFIX	A suffix is added to the end of the word to make a new word.
SYMBOLISM	The use of symbols to represent an idea or quality.
SYNONYM	A word that has the same or similar meaning to another word.
TRADITIONAL LITERATURE	The oldest type of literature. Stories passed down from generation to generation.
VERB	A verb is a *doing* or *action* word.

UNDERSTANDING FICTION

UNDERSTANDING FICTION

WHAT IS FICTION?

Fiction is the creation of stories and ideas. They are created by the IMAGINATION.

These stories are NOT real.

If you've read our other Key Stage 2 books, you will have been introduced to our superhero characters. If not, let me quickly go over who they are!

We have Preston, Scarlett, Freddie, Lalita and Anil.

Like I said, when talking about fiction, we are talking about stories that are made up. Our superhero characters are a great example of this – they have been created through the use of our imagination. They are not real, they are simply imaginary.

TYPES OF FICTION

There are many different types of fiction books:

Fantasy	Romance	Horror	Science Fiction (Sci-Fi)
Mystery	Realistic	Historical	Folktales
Adventure	Sports	Humour	Classics

Some fiction stories use more than one **genre**, and this is called a **hybrid**.

UNDERSTANDING FICTION

EXAMPLES OF CLASSIC CHILDREN'S FICTION

There are so many children's books out there by different authors, from different genres.

Entering the world of pure imagination and original thoughts will allow children to expand on their own creative ideas.

Below I have listed some of the most classic children's fiction books. When you have some time, I would recommend that you read some of these before your English SAT.

Alice in Wonderland	Treasure Island	The Railway Children	Black Beauty
A Little Princess	The Secret Garden	The Wizard of Oz	The Lion, the Witch, and the Wardrobe
Peter Pan	Watership Down	The Indian in the Cupboard	Charlotte's Web
The Borrowers	Annie	Wind in the Willows	Charlie and the Chocolate Factory

A GOOD FICTION BOOK

When reading a story it is important that you can be drawn into the story, escape from the real world and enter a realm of fantasy and make-believe.

On the other hand, as the creator/writer of fiction, you need to be able to tell a story that will engage your readers.

<u>Every good fiction book, comes with:</u>

- *A creative imagination;*
- *An original idea;*
- *A strong narrative;*
- *Characters that people can relate to, disapprove of, or admire;*
- *An ability to look beyond reality and enter a world of vision, fantasy, and invention.*

UNDERSTANDING FICTION

READING COMPLEX FICTION

The best advice that I can give to you is to read as many different *types* of books as you can.

While it's great to find a genre you love, only sticking to one may limit your ability to expand your knowledge.

By reading books from different authors, genres and eras, you will be able to see how writing styles differ from one another, and how each written text uses particular techniques in order to draw in their readers.

Improve your reading ability by:

- ✓ Reading books from different authors.
- ✓ Reading books from different genres.
- ✓ Reading books from different eras *(traditional vs. modern).*

QUESTIONING THE TEXT

It is important that, after reading the text, you think about what has been written.

You need to be able to read an extract from a book, and understand the passage in further detail.

By asking questions as you go through, this will allow you to understand what the author was trying to say:

- *How does the author want me to feel at this point?*
- *How does the author feel at this point?*
- *Why have I been provided this information?*
- *What can I learn from the information that has been provided?*
- *Why has the author used a particular phrase?*
- *Who is the narrator of the text and how are they being portrayed?*

UNDERSTANDING FICTION

LANGUAGE AND MEANING

Everyone knows that English is an extremely complicated language. There are so many rules to writing, that it makes it difficult to understand what is actually being said.

You need to be able to learn the meaning of words which can be used in different contexts. For example, a word that was used 50 years ago might have a different meaning in today's world.

You will need to identify these types of words and understand the correct meaning, in relation to the passage it is written in. This will allow you to improve your comprehensive skills and therefore score higher in your English SATs.

	MEANING 1	MEANING 2
Sick	'Ill' or 'unwell'	'Amazing' or 'cool'
Cell	'Jail' or 'body cells'	'Mobile phone'
Naughty	'Poor' or 'nothing'	'Badly behaved'

Can you think of any other words that use to mean something, but is now used to mean something else?

UNDERSTANDING FICTION

LANGUAGE AND CONTEXT

Another thing to consider in relation to language and meaning, is the context in which a story is set.

The language of a book contributes to the overall tone of the author. This is done on purpose. The author uses specific language in order to 'fit' with the time and place in which the book was set.

Let me explain this in more detail:

- In the USA, the writing style is very different to that of British authors. Americans would use words such as *garbage can* (dustbin), *soccer* (football), *vacation* (holiday), *sidewalk* (pavement) and many more words.

See how the language changes?

PRESENTATION AND MEANING

Language is not the only important element when it comes to writing. **Presentation** is key when writing a story.

Some fiction books, particularly in children's books, use pictures alongside the written content. This is done for a reason; it allows the reader to visualise people or objects, as opposed to just reading what they look like.

When it comes to presentation, there are a few things you should pay attention to:

- Facial expressions;
- Body language;
- Background setting;
- Costumes and props.

How would you describe our superhero, Freddie?

UNDERSTANDING FICTION

THE KEY ELEMENTS OF FICTION WRITING

Below I have outlined the key elements of what makes a good fiction book:

➢ CHARACTERS

The characters of a story are extremely significant as they allow the reader to follow the lives of made-up individuals. The way in which a character comes across to readers is through **characterisation**.

The author would have given each character a certain look, personality traits and behaviour attributes. This allows the reader to understand and visualise the characters in a bit more detail, which would simply go unnoticed or forgotten otherwise.

➢ SETTING

The setting of a story allows the reader to be drawn in to what is happening, and where it is all taking place. Authors can be really descriptive when it comes to settings, and they do this for one main reason; they want their readers to be able to escape from their real lives and enter a world of pure imagination.

Not only does describing settings prove to be invaluable in terms of creative thinking, but it also allows the author to create a particular *feel* to the writing. The era the narrative is set in can be identified by explaining everything around the characters.

➢ NARRATIVE

Behind every great fiction book is a strong narrative that draws the reader in, and captures a story that is thrilling and appealing to its targeted readers.

The narrative is where the author can get really creative. Remember, fiction writing is all about fantasy and make-believe. Therefore, the ideas and imagination behind these stories can be completely unrealistic and wacky.

UNDERSTANDING FICTION

ANALYSING FICTION

One of the main elements of English Comprehension assessments is to determine your ability to read a piece of text and then **analyse** the information.

Literary analysis is focusing on the characters, plotline, setting and language in order to understand the meaning put across by the author. Remember, the author has written the text with the intention of coming across in a certain light. Your job is to work out what the author means by everything they have written.

When analysing passages, you will often be asked questions in the style of:

- Using examples;
- Drawing inferences;
- Making predictions.

Using examples – when answering questions, it is important that you **support** your answer with EVIDENCE.

Evidence: words and sentences that you take DIRECTLY from the passage. Anything that you have quoted from the passage will need to be written in quotation marks (see definitions).

Drawing inferences – You might be asked a question where you have to state a conclusion based on the information provided.

An inference is merely a conclusion based on evidence and reasoning. For example, if you were told "Jimmie went straight to the fridge as soon as he got in from school", you could infer that Jimmie was hungry.

Even though the conclusion might not necessarily be one hundred percent spot on, it is definitely something you can assume based on the information provided.

Making predictions – sometimes you might be asked to predict what might happen. The author will often provide hints or clues in their writing that might make you think, "I know how this is going to end".

Stories that are unpredictable are enjoyable to most readers because they offer mystery and suspense; they keep the reader wanting more.

Read the passage carefully and answer the following questions.

Extract from *Freddie and the Stolen Ring* by How2Become.

"It's gone!"

Freddie looked up from peering through one of the glass cabinets, hoping to find the perfect item of jewellery for his best friend, Scarlett. He was in a small jewellery shop in the city centre of CapeTown. The walls were painted in a dark red, with pictures hung crookedly all around. The floor was tiled and scuffed. The harsh lighting made it difficult to see what you were looking at, but somehow it made it feel cosier, more inviting.

Freddie stood in the farthest corner away from the tills, but the sound of the trembling young girl grabbed his attention. No older than 20, the young girl paced around the shop with her phone fixed to her ear, trying to report the incident. As customers stopped in their tracks to ogle the spectacle, the shop was beginning to overflow with curiosity and interest.

Once admired for his vigilance and passion, all Freddie could do now was stand there frozen, contemplating his next move. It had been exactly 3 years. How could he possibly forget it? 3 years since Freddie's accident, and he had found himself in a quandary since that unforgettable day.

"I don't know what happened...one minute it was there, and the next it was gone – the ring is gone".

As moments passed, Freddie knew what had to be done. He couldn't stand by and do nothing. *Come on, you can do it! Just think, think!* He kept reassuring himself, and as he closed his eyes, his body started to tremble. The black nothingness started to get brighter. Reds and oranges began penetrating his vision. These colours then formed distorted images. Images of the ring. *Where, where is it?* Freddie said to himself.

Freddie was known for his excellent vision to read minds and see into the future. However, he had refrained from doing this since his accident, and the feeling of entering this state of mind after so much time made his body go limp.

He opened his eyes, pupils dilated. They were so intense that the strongest gust of wind would not have made him blink. Slowly, Freddie reached into his pocket and pulled out what appeared to be a torch. With his eyes still transfixed, he clicked the button. After a few seconds, he clicked it again.

Now stood there, was a man all in green. A long, silk cape which hovered above the floor, an eye mask that made his eyes look as black as coal, and boots that, although appeared to look 'normal', had hidden features that placed him in a very strong position against all odds.

"It's time…It's time to get back to solving crime!"

Freddie had not realised how loud he said this, and as he turned around, he noticed everyone staring at him, silently. He grinned slightly.

"I've got this…"

Question 1

Using **evidence** from the extract, describe the jewellery shop.

____

____

____

Question 2

The author uses the phrase 'in a quandary'. What does this mean?

____

____

____

Question 3

What can you infer from the extract? Circle **one**.

That everyone is being held hostage.	That Freddie is a superhero.	That Freddie is the robber.	That the police have arrested the robber.

Question 4

The word 'normal' is written in quotation marks. Why do you think the author has done this? Tick **one**.

To suggest that the boots are for normal, everyday use. ☐

To suggest that the author is being sarcastic. ☐

To suggest that the boots have special powers. ☐

To suggest that the author has made a mistake. ☐

Question 5

The author uses a simile in the extract. Write the exact words of the simile.

____

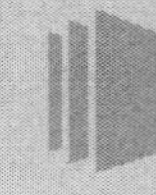

Question 6

The author uses the **adjectives** “trembling” and “distorted”. Give a definition of each of these words.

Trembling

Meaning:

____

____

Distorted

Meaning:

____

____

Question 7

Freddie needs your help. The author claims that all Freddie could do was “stand there frozen”. Which of the following best describes this phrase? Tick **one**.

Literal ☐

Figurative ☐

Allegorical ☐

Sarcasm ☐

Question 8

In the first paragraph, the author describes the jewellery shop. Give **two** possible reasons why the author might have done this.

Question 9

On more than one occasion, the author uses ellipses in their writing. Explain the use of an ellipsis, using an example from the extract.

Question 10

How long was it since Freddie's accident?

12 months	24 months	36 months	40 months

Question 11

The author uses the phrase, "How could he possibly forget it?" What does the author mean by this?

Question 12

The author ends the extract with the phrase, “I’ve got this...” What do you suppose the author means by this?

____

____

____

Question 13

The author uses the word “ogle”. Out of the following, which sentence best defines this term? Tick **one**.

Taking a quick glance. ☐

To stare at the event in an interested manner. ☐

To show a lack of interest. ☐

To show a rude and disrespectful attitude. ☐

Question 14

The author uses the word “spectacle”. From reading the extract, what or who is the author describing as the “spectacle”? Circle **one**.

The customers	The robber	The incident	The young girl

Question 15

Write down three quotes from the extract, which allow the reader to 'get to know' Freddie.

1. ______________________________

____

2. ______________________________

____

3. ______________________________

____

Read the passage carefully and answer the following questions.

Extract from *Webster and his Journey Home* by How2Become.

Strand by strand, Webster created an intricate infrastructure; a structure so defined and carefully constructed, that it made all others seem unrefined. Clear light lines that, although appeared fragile and breakable, were actually a strong, valuable asset to the world in which he lived.

"It's all in the spinning," Webster smiled as he continued to finish off his masterpiece. There was nothing Webster liked doing more than spending time with his companion, Toby. Together they would create a sense of security and triumph – Webster's definition of perfection.

On the surface, Webster appeared to be like any other of his kind; a dark shade of brown, with legs as fast as they could carry. Webster was just ordinary, nothing special, nothing different; just blending in with the rest of the crowd.

Webster would move from place to place, doing the same things he had always done. He knew no other way; it was a routine thing for him. A routine that would eventually get him home. He had become complacent with his way of life. He knew that every 'man' was out for himself, and although the rest of them would have learnt to protect and hide themselves in their patterned shelter, Webster felt the need to be ridiculously excessive. After all, he was tiny and suffered with a damaged leg, all of which made him inferior to the leader of the cluster.

Today's the day, Webster kept reciting to himself. *Today's the day I finally go home*. Webster had been waiting for this day for quite some time. Since the day he got separated from his family back in New York. He could remember the day like it was just yesterday. The smell of freshly cut grass from Central Park, fused with the scent of petroleum and food shops.

Webster made his way through the streets, minding his step and remaining on high alert for danger. *Not long now! Not long at all!*

"I'm quite lucky, really. I mean… my life has been pretty cool despite everything. Put it this way, I would never have met you, Toby."

Can you imagine? The thought of not knowing Toby seemed practically impossible to Webster. Toby was Webster's best friend. They went everywhere together. They were like two peas in a pod.

According to Webster's calculations, it would take about an hour and a half to reach his destination. Despite waiting for this day, Webster was uncertain. Uncertain on whether or not his family would still be there; whether his family were still alive; whether things would be different.

A split second of horror filled Webster's thoughts. He stopped in his tracks. He turned slightly and faced a shop window. The shop appeared to have been abandoned for quite some time, with grime and dust spread all over the window.

"What if they don't like me, Tobz? What would I do then?"

As Webster stood looking into the dusty window, he slowly wiped the window clear. There he stood, looking at himself. He took note of the time on the clock – 6:15pm.

After a moment's glance, Webster was no longer fearful of the thought of his family, but the thought that Toby, his beloved companion, had no reflection.

Question 1

Why do you think the author has used the name "Webster"? What **inference** can we make from this choice of name?

____

____

Question 2

List three examples of how you know the author is implying the above (as answered in question 1).

1. ____

____

2. ____

____

3. ____

____

Question 3

The author uses the phrase, "a structure so defined and carefully constructed, that it made all others seem unrefined". What do you believe the author is referring to here?

____

Question 4

What nickname does Webster give Toby?

____

Question 5

What is Webster's definition of perfection? Use **evidence** to support your answer.

Question 6

Write **two** of the similes and explain the importance of why the author has used that literary technique.

Simile 1

Explanation

Simile 2

Explanation

Question 7

In which form of narration is *Webster and his Journey Home* written?

1st person	2nd person	3rd person	All of them

Question 8

Lalita needs your help identifying literary techniques. The author uses the phrase, *"Can you imagine?"* What type of literary technique is this? Tick **one**.

Metaphor ☐

Analogy ☐

Bathos ☐

Rhetorical question ☐

Question 9

The author ends the extract with the sentence, "After a moment's glance, Webster was no longer fearful of the thought of his family, but the thought that Toby, his beloved companion, had no reflection."

What can you **infer** from the sentence above?

____

____

____

____

How do you think the author would describe Webster's feelings after this discovery?

____

____

____

____

Question 10

Explain why the author creates the character of Toby. How does this make the reader feel in regards to Webster?

Question 11

The author states **two** reasons as to why Webster's "masterpiece" is resourceful. Find the **evidence** in the passage and then write it out word-for-word.

Reason 1

Reason 2

Question 12

The author talks about Webster's memory in regards to the day he got separated from his family. Why do you think the author has done this?

Question 13

The author uses the word "cool" to talk about Webster's experience of life. There are two meanings to this term. Fill in the boxes below to demonstrate how the word is used in this context, and how it could be used in a different context.

	Extract context	**Alternative context**
"Cool"		

Question 14

If Webster's calculations are correct, what time would he arrive at his destination? Circle **one**.

18:45 **17:30** **19:45** **21:35**

Question 15

Describe the contrast in which the author makes between paragraph 1 and paragraph 3. Give **examples** of how the author has conveyed this contrast.

____

____

____

____

____

____

Read the passage carefully and answer the following questions.

Extract from *The Wonderful Wizard of Oz* by L. Frank Baum.

"What makes you a coward?" asked Dorothy, looking at the great beast in wonder, for he was as big as a small horse.

"It's a mystery," replied the Lion. "I suppose I was born that way. All the other animals in the forest naturally expect me to be brave, for the Lion is everywhere thought to be the King of Beasts. I learned that if I roared very loudly every living thing was frightened and got out of my way. Whenever I've met a man I've been awfully scared; but I just roared at him, and he has always run away as fast as he could go. If the elephants and the tigers and the bears had ever tried to fight me, I should have run myself – I'm such a coward; but just as soon as they hear me roar they all try to get away from me and of course I let them go."

"But that isn't right. The King of Beasts shouldn't be a coward," said the Scarecrow.

"I know it," returned the Lion, wiping a tear from his eye with the tip of his tail; "it is my great sorrow, and makes my life very unhappy. But whenever there is danger my heart begins to beat fast."

"Perhaps you have heart disease," said the Tin Woodman.

"It may be," said the Lion.

"If you have," continued the Tin Woodman, "you ought to be glad, for it proves you have a heart. For my part, I have no heart; so I cannot have heart disease."

"Perhaps," said the Lion, thoughtfully, "if I had no heart I should not be a coward."

"Have you brains?" asked the Scarecrow.

"I suppose so. I've never looked to see," replied the Lion.

"I am going to the great Oz to ask him to give me some," remarked the Scarecrow, "for my head is stuffed with straw."

"And I am going to ask him to give me a heart," said the Woodman.

"And I am going to ask him to send Toto and me back to Kansas," added Dorothy.

"Do you think Oz could give me courage?" asked the cowardly Lion.

"Just as easily as he could give me brains," said the Scarecrow.

"Or give me a heart," said the Tin Woodman.

"Or send me back to Kansas," said Dorothy.

"Then, if you don't mind, I'll go with you," said the Lion, "for my life is simply unbearable without a bit of courage."

"You will be very welcome," answered Dorothy, "for you will help to keep away the other wild beasts. It seems to me they must be more cowardly than you are if they allow you to scare them so easily."

"They really are," said the Lion; "but that doesn't make me any braver, and as long as I know myself to be a coward I shall be unhappy."

So once more the little company set off upon the journey, the Lion walking with stately strides at Dorothy's side. Toto did not approve this new comrade at first, for he could not forget how nearly he had been crushed between the Lion's great jaws; but after a time he became more at ease, and presently Toto and the Cowardly Lion had grown to be friends.

Question 1

If you were to perform this extract on stage, what characters would you need in order to complete the scene?

Question 2

Write down, using **evidence** from the extract, what each character wants to ask the great Oz.

Dorothy

Scarecrow

Lion

Tin Woodman

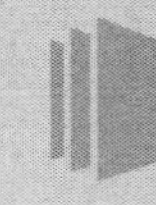

Question 3

What adjective is used to describe the Lion? Circle **one**.

Curious	Cowardly	Ugly	Aggressive

Write the definition of the word that you have circled.

____

____

____

Question 4

What synonyms for the word "said" does the author use in this extract?

____

____

____

Question 5

What simile is used to describe the appearance of the Lion?

____

____

Question 6

What makes the Lion's heart beat faster? Why do you think the author provides the reader with this information?

____

____

____

Question 7

The author uses the phrase, "King of Beasts". Which of the following best summarises the use of this phrase, in context of the passage? Tick **one**.

The Scarecrow should be the most superior in the forest. ☐

The Lion should be viewed as aggressive and strong. ☐

The Lion should be the most superior in the forest. ☐

Dorothy is afraid when meeting the Lion for the first time. ☐

Question 8

The author continuously makes reference to the Lion as being cowardly. However the Lions physical description is of a fearful "beast". Which literary technique is the author conveying? Circle **one**.

Anecdote	Irony	Colloquialism	Exaggeration

Question 9

Anil needs your help. The author uses the phrase, "stately strides" to describe the Lion's walk. Which of the following gives the best definition of this phrase?

Slow, grand and decisive steps. ☐

Quick-paced power walk. ☐

Heavy, long stomps. ☐

Walking with a scuff. ☐

Question 10

List all of the words or phrases you can find in the above extract to convey the Lion's unhappiness.

______

______

______

______

______

______

Question 11

The author uses the words "company" and "comrade" to emphasise a particular point. What reasons could the author have for describing the group using military language?

______

______

______

Question 12

How do you know Dorothy is not afraid of the Lion, whom she looks at in great "wonder"?

______

______

______

Question 13

Throughout the extract, the author implies that Tin Woodman has no heart. However, he tries to reassure the Lion by telling him he "ought to be glad."

What do you think the author is trying to do here?

Question 14

Throughout the extract, the author implies that the Scarecrow has no brains. Which sentence in the extract could contradict this idea?

Question 15

Which of the characters in the extract do you sympathise with the most? Use evidence from the passage in order to strengthen your reasoning.

Read the passage carefully and answer the following questions.

Extract from *Alice's Adventures in Wonderland* by Lewis Carroll.

There seemed to be no use in waiting by the little door, so she went back to the table, half hoping she might find another key on it, or at any rate a book of rules for shutting people up like telescopes: this time she found a little bottle on it, ('which certainly was not here before,' said Alice,) and tied round the neck of the bottle was a paper label with the words 'DRINK ME' beautifully printed on it in large letters.

It was all very well to say 'Drink me,' but the wise, little Alice was not going to do *that* in a hurry: 'no I'll look first,' she said, 'and see whether it's marked "*poison*" or not:' for she had read several nice little stories about children who had got burnt, and eaten up by wild beasts, and other unpleasant things, all because they *would* not remember the simple rules their friends had taught them, such as, that a red-hot poker will burn you if you hold it too long; and that if you cut your finger *very* deeply with a knife, it usually bleeds; and she had never forgotten that, if you drink much from a bottle marked 'poison,' it is almost certain to disagree with you, sooner or later.

However, this bottle was *not* marked 'poison,' so Alice ventured to taste it and finding it very nice, (it had, in fact, a sort of mixed flavour of cherry-tart, custard, pine-apple, roast turkey, toffee, and hot buttered toast,) she very soon finished it off.

'What a curious feeling!' said Alice; 'I must be shutting up like a telescope.'

And so it was indeed: she was now only ten inches high, and her face brightened up at the thought that she was now the right size for going through the little door into that lovely garden. First, however, she waited for a few minutes to see if she was going to shrink any further: she felt a little nervous about this, 'for it might end, you know,' said Alice to herself, 'in my going out altogether, like a candle. I wonder what I should be like then?' And she tried to fancy what the flame of a candle looks like after the candle is blown out, for she could not remember ever having seen such a thing.

After a while, finding that nothing more had happened, she decided on going into the garden at once. But, alas for poor Alice! when she got to the door, she found she had forgotten the little golden key, and when she went back to the table for it, she found she could not possibly reach it: she could see it quite plainly through the glass, and she tried her best to climb up one of the legs of the table, but it was too slippery, and when she had tired herself out with trying, the poor little thing sat down and cried.

'Come, there's no use in crying like that!' said Alice to herself, rather sharply, 'I advise you to leave off this minute!' She generally gave herself very good advice, (though she very seldom followed it), and sometimes she scolded herself so severely as to bring tears into her eyes, and once she remembered trying to box her own ears for having cheated herself in a game of croquet she was playing against herself, for this curious child was very fond of pretending to be two people. 'But it's no use now,' thought poor Alice, 'to pretend to be two people! Why, there's hardly enough of me left to make *one* respectable person!'

Question 1

How would you describe the character of Alice?

Question 2

The author of this book portrays Alice as a curious little girl. Find **two** references from the extract, and explain how the author's language shapes our views about Alice.

Reference 1

Reference 2

Question 3

The author makes reference to changes in Alice's physical description. Using **examples** from the text, why do you think the author does this and what does this tell us about the character of Alice?

____

____

____

____

____

____

Question 4

Number the below references from the passage, in order in which they happened.

Alice sits down and cries. ☐

Alice realises that she has forgotten the key. ☐

Alice shrinks. ☐

Alice tries to climb the table. ☐

Alice drinks the bottle. ☐

Question 5

Do you think that Alice should have drunk the bottle on the table? Circle **yes** or **no**.

YES **NO**

Give reasons for your answer, using the information from the extract.

____

____

____

____

____

____

____

____

____

Question 6

What does Alice compare herself to when she realises she is shrinking? Give the exact phrase.

____

____

Question 7

After drinking from the bottle, what still prevented Alice from going through the door? Circle **one**.

She was too big	She forgot where the door was	She forgot the key	She was too scared

Question 8

In the extract, the author makes reference to a key and a door. The author has used this object to not only fit in with the storyline, but to act as a symbol.

What could the key and door be symbolic for and how does this fit in with the narrative so far?

Question 9

The author describes how Alice would feel if she was unable to continue her adventures. The author compares this to "what the flame of a candle looks like after the candle is blown out". Why do you think the author has made the comparison between Alice's adventures and a flaming candle?

Question 10

Give a **possible** explanation as to why the author might have described the main character as someone who "was very fond of pretending to be two people".

Question 11

The author uses the term "scolded" when describing Alice at the end of the extract. Which of the following sentences best defines this term? Tick **one**.

Alice knows that if her mum was there, she would be punished for acting childishly. ☐

Alice believes that she is unworthy of continuing on with her journey. ☐

Alice disciplines herself when she believes she's done something wrong. ☐

Alice likes the attention she gets when she cries, so disciplining herself is a way of receiving that much needed attention. ☐

Question 12

What do you think the author means by the phrase, "shutting people up like telescopes"?

____

____

____

____

Question 13

The author makes reference to a garden in the above extract. What do you think the garden represents? Why do you think the author has done this?

____

____

____

____

Question 14

The author uses the term "long". This has two connotations. In context of the passage, it shows how holding something for a *long* time can get you burnt. However, another use of the word is this idea of *longing* for something.

Explain how the extract demonstrates Alice *longing* for something. Use **evidence** to support your answer.

Question 15

Freddie has an important question for you. From reading the extract, what themes or common motifs are displayed? Why do you think the author has done this? Use **examples** to support your answer.

ANSWERS TO FICTION

Freddie and the Stolen Ring

Q1. The jewellery shop can be described as being small which is located "in the city centre of CapeTown. The walls were painted in a dark red, with pictures hung crookedly all around. The floor was tiled and scuffed. The harsh lighting made it difficult to see what you were looking at."

(Remember, this question specifically asks you to use evidence. Therefore, you need to quote from the actual text. Don't forget to use quotation marks).

Q2. The phrase "in a quandary" means uncertainty. Freddie was unsure of his next move, and therefore found himself in a difficult predicament.

(You should try to improve your vocabulary by understanding the meaning of different words).

Q3. 'That Freddie is a superhero'.

(Although the author does not actually state this, the way in which Freddie is described, suggests superhero characteristics such as "he couldn't stand by and do nothing". His clothing of a long, silk cape and an eye mask also suggests that he is a superhero. Finally, the phrase "it's time to get back to solving crime", makes it even more obvious that he is, in fact, a superhero).

Q4. To suggest that the boots have special powers.

Q5. "His eyes look as black as coal."

(A simile is used to describe one thing and compare it to the likes of another).

Q6. Trembling = shaking with fear, anxiousness or vulnerability. The young girl is described as trembling after the robbery, therefore she is most likely feeling scared and vulnerable.

Distorted = an image made to look out of shape and deformed. It is unclear and therefore makes it hard to define. When Freddie is visualising the ring, the images are distorted i.e. they are blurred or out of shape.

Q7. Figurative

(Figurative language is a figure of speech that goes beyond the literal meaning. For example, metaphors, similes, hyperboles, personification. Figurative language is used metaphorically).

Q8. The author has described the jewellery shop because it sets the scene and allows the reader to get a sense of where they are. The readers are instantly brought into the story by being able to visualise the scenery. Also, the author has described the jewellery shop because this is the place where the main incident takes place – it is part of the storyline.

Q9. An ellipsis is used to create suspense, or leave a sentence purposely unfinished. For example, the author uses an ellipsis in the sentence, "It's time... It's time to get back to solving crime". The author has used the ellipsis there to emphasise a pause in speech. This creates suspense and makes the writing more dramatic.

Q10. 36 months

(The passage tells us that "It had been exactly 3 years". 3 years is equivalent to 36 months).

Q11. The author uses the phrase, "How could he possibly forget?" in order to draw upon memories, memories that are embedded into his mind. The author is talking about Freddie's accident. The author suggests that Freddie is unable to forget because it is a significant event that has impacted his life.

Q12. The author ends the passage with the phrase, "I've got this..." to suggest that Freddie is going to resolve the robbery and find out who has stolen the ring. He will be the hero.

Q13. To stare at the event in an interested manner.

(Ogle can be defined as staring or gazing at something with great interest).

Q14. The incident

(The author describes the incident as a spectacle. The passage states, "As customers stopped in their tracks to ogle the spectacle", this suggests that the customers found something interesting to look at, which in this case, was the robbery).

Q15. Quote 1 = "3 years since Freddie's accident" – This gives the reader some background information about Freddie's life. Freddie has suffered an accident which is ultimately affecting his decision regarding his next steps after the robbery.

Quote 2 = "his excellent vision to read minds and see into the future" – This tells the reader about how powerful Freddie is. It tells the reader that he has superhero features.

Quote 3 = "It's time...It's time to get back to solving crime!" – This reiterates that Freddie is a superhero. The reader will know that the rest of the story will be based on Freddie finding the stolen ring, and this should hopefully keep the reader wanting to know how it will turn out.

Webster and his Journey Home

Q1. The author has used the name 'Webster' to imply that he is, in fact, a spider.

Q2. *"Webster created an intricate infrastructure; a structure so defined and carefully constructed"* – this is talking about the spider's web.

"He knew that every 'man' was out for himself" – 'man' is written in inverted commas, suggesting that Webster is not actually a man.

"After all, he was tiny and suffered with a damaged leg, all of which made him inferior to the leader of the cluster." – The term 'cluster' is used to describe a group of spiders.

Q3. The author uses the phrase, "a structure so defined and carefully constructed, that it made all others seem unrefined". This is clearly talking about a spider's web and how they are carefully created.

Q4. Tobz

(These types of question are asking you to re-read the passage and pinpoint specific information).

Q5. Webster's definition of perfection is, "Together they would create a sense of security and triumph". At this point, Webster is talking about creating a spider's web and this is what he is referring to in regards to perfection.

(The question asks you to support your answer. You need to use direct quotes from the passage in order to score high marks).

Q6. "They were like two peas in a pod" – this simile is showing the close relationship formed between Webster and Toby; they are inseparable.

"With legs as fast as they would carry" – this is conveying how the spider moves as fast as he possibly can.

Q7. 3rd person

Q8. Rhetorical question

(A rhetorical question is a question that you ask without requiring an answer).

Q9. You can infer that Webster's friend, Toby, does not exist. The fact that Toby had "no reflection", suggests that he is imaginary.

When Webster realises this, you could expect him to feel upset, lonely, and maybe slightly confused. His beloved companion that he's shared his life with is non-existent, so Webster would be emotionally damaged, and would need some time to come to terms with the situation. After all, it's just like losing someone, even if they never existed in the first place.

Q10. The author creates the character of Toby to allow you to understand the character of Webster in a bit more detail. The fact that Webster has imagined him, shows that he is lonely and seeking companionship; something that he lost when he was separated from his family.

Q11. "Create a sense of security and triumph"

"Protect and hide themselves"

Q12. The author talks about the memories Webster has before he got separated from his family, because it allows the reader to sympathise with his character. It allows a bit of background information to be added to the character of Webster.

Q13.

	Extract context	**Alternative context**
"Cool"	To show that it was 'great', 'amazing' or 'fun.	A low temperature.

Q14. 19:45

Q15. The contrast between light and dark is being made between paragraphs 1 and 3. In the first paragraph, the author talks about the "clear light lines" which make up a spider's web. Conversely, in paragraph 3, the author discusses the appearance of Webster as being "a dark shade of brown". This has been done to create a clear distinction. The light lines could represent fragility and vulnerability, whereas the dark brown could represent nature and stability.

The Wonderful Wizard of Oz

Q1. Dorothy, Toto, Lion, Scarecrow, Tin Woodman

Q2. Dorothy = "And I am going to ask him to send Toto and me back to Kansas".

Scarecrow = "And I am going to the great Oz to ask him to give me some (brains)…for my head is stuffed with straw".

Lion = "Do you think Oz could give me courage?"

Tin Woodman = "And I am going to ask him to give me a heart".

Q3. Cowardly

A coward is someone who lacks the courage to do dangerous, conflicting or unpleasant things.

Q4. Asked, replied, returned, remarked, continued, added, answered

Q5. "As big as a small horse"

Q6. Danger makes the Lion's heart beat faster. The reason he is asking for courage when he gets to the great Oz is so that he is not afraid of danger and can be brave when it comes to handling confrontations.

Q7. The Lion should be the most superior in the forest.

Q8. Irony

(There is irony in the fact that the Lion is considered to be King of the Beasts, yet lacks courage. Irony is displaying one meaning but conveying the complete opposite).

Q9. Slow, grand and decisive steps

Q10. Awfully scared, wiping a tear from his eye, sorrow, unhappy

Q11. The use of the words "company" and "comrade" are used to emphasise a bond between the characters. This bond demonstrates that the group are *like* a military in the sense that they show strength, motivation, loyalty to each other and teamwork.

Q12. You can tell that Dorothy is not scared of the Lion because she looks at him in great "wonder"; she does not look at him with fear. She also allows him to accompany them to Oz to grant all of their wishes.

Q13. The fact that Tin Woodman wants a heart so that he can 'feel' something, conflicts with Woodman's statement that, "you ought to be glad". This in itself shows that the Tin man already has feelings because he is showing empathy towards the Lion. The word "glad" suggests that he already recognises/feels emotions, which could imply that he already has a heart.

Q14. "But this isn't right. The King of Beasts shouldn't be a coward". This suggests that the Scarecrow already has brains because he is showing knowledge about what King of Beasts should not be like.

Q15. *This question relies on personal response. You can choose any character so long as you support your reasons with evidence from the passage.*

(For example, you could argue that the Lion is the character you sympathise with most because the passage talks a lot about his feelings and unhappiness about not being brave. You could support your answer with phrases such as, "wiping a tear from his eye", "it is my great sorrow" and "as long as I know myself to be a coward I shall be unhappy").

Alice's Adventures in Wonderland

Q1. Alice can be described as a curious young girl who is seeking an exciting new adventure. This is demonstrated through the use of words such as "curious" and "ventured".

Q2. "This bottle was not marked 'poison,' so Alice ventured to taste it". – This shows Alice's curiosity as all it takes for her to drink from the bottle is a quick check that the word 'poison' is not written on it. Her desire to find out what was in the bottle overwhelms any sense of caution she might have had about the unknown substance.

"When she got to the door, she found she had forgotten the little golden key" – This shows Alice's curiosity as she is trying to use the door to enter into the unknown.

Q3. The author conveys Alice's character in different sizes – small and normal-sized. This is emphasised when she drinks the potion and shrinks to "ten inches tall". The author does this to illustrate fantasy; "I must be shutting up like a telescope". This could not happen in real life and therefore it's all in the imagination. The author might have done this to show that Alice is not comfortable with who she is. For example, she has to change into a different version of herself in order to find happiness.

Q4.

Alice sits down and cries.	**5**
Alice realises that she has forgotten the key.	**3**
Alice shrinks.	**2**
Alice tries to climb the table.	**4**
Alice drinks the bottle.	**1**

Q5. *This question relies on personal response. You can choose either yes or no, as long as you support your reasons with evidence from the passage.*

(For example, you could argue yes for whether Alice should have drunk the potion. You could support your answer by explaining how Alice is a "curious" young girl and seeks adventure. Finding the "key" and unlocking the door is a way of her finding out more about who she is. The use of the word "telescopes" suggests that there is more to see, and she wants to find a new perspective. These are all reasons for why Alice should have drunk the potion.)

Q6. "I must be shutting up like a telescope"

Q7. She forgot the key

Q8. The key could be used as a symbol for Alice's imagination. Alice is trying to unlock the door to enter a world of pure imagination. The door could represent the barrier between real life and fantasy. It could also represent the entrance and exit to happiness; opening up new experiences and adventures.

Q9. The significance of the candle burning out is compared to Alice wanting to finish her adventures. A dying out candle represents Alice's feelings if she is unable to continue on with her adventures.

Q10. The author describes the main character, Alice, as someone who is "very fond of pretending to be two people". This could be because Alice is unhappy with who she is, and is trying to be someone else. It shows that Alice has a creative imagination and is able to gain a new perspective.

Q11. Alice disciplines herself when she believes she's done something wrong.

Q12. The phrase, "shutting people up like telescopes" is most likely referring to making someone smaller. "Shutting up" doesn't necessarily mean to make someone quiet, but to "shut up" i.e. to make smaller, like a telescope when its put away after being used.

Q13. The garden could be representing beauty and innocence. It could also be representing freedom and desire. The garden is created through the use of imagination and therefore the garden could suggest that Alice is trying to relive her childhood and maintain her innocent and naïve manner.

Q14. The extract is about the idea for *longing* for something. Alice is longing to find adventure and desire. She is longing to keep her childhood alive through the use of creativeness and imagination. When the author talks about Alice "pretending to be two people", this suggests that Alice is longing for something else, i.e. to be someone different or experience something new.

Q15. *This question relies on personal response. You need to read the passage carefully and see what themes or motifs are being displayed.*

(For example, themes you could talk about could include holding on to childhood, conquests – trying to work her way through her imagination which encounters all types of obstacles. Motifs include dreams and fantasy, curiosity and vulnerability).

HOW ARE YOU GETTING ON?

WRITING YOUR OWN FICTION

WRITING YOUR OWN FICTION

A great way to practice for your English Comprehension assessment, is to undergo your own writing tasks.

In this chapter, I am going to talk you through how to create successful stories, and provide you with some useful tips to improve your writing ability.

STRUCTURING YOUR STORY

The first thing you need to understand is that the structure of your story is important. It allows the reader to be engaged instantly, and be kept excited until the very end.

Every story has a beginning, middle and end:

BEGINNING

- Introducing your reader to your style of writing.
- Setting up the scene and introducing the main characters.
- Creating a 'situation' or 'problem' right at the beginning will make sure that your reader is instantly 'hooked'.
- You need to grab the reader's attention. Make it thrilling. Make it fast-paced. Make the reader want to continue reading.
- Don't give away all of the key details at the beginning. Provide your readers with enough information, so that they will want to continue reading on to find out more.

MIDDLE

- This is where the bulk of your story will take place.
- You need to hold the reader's attention by maintaining a plotline that is interesting, and will push the reader to finish the story.
- Develop obstacles and complications which the characters need to solve.
- Although there might be a few complications, your story should reach a CLIMAX or turning point.
- There is a massive situation which the main character has to try and resolve.
- A good middle will allow the reader to wonder how the story will end.

END

- This is where the climax or turning point of your story will become resolved.
- Your main character/s will have learnt a lesson, or come to terms with the events that have happened.
- A good ending will allow the reader to continue thinking about the story, even after finishing reading it.

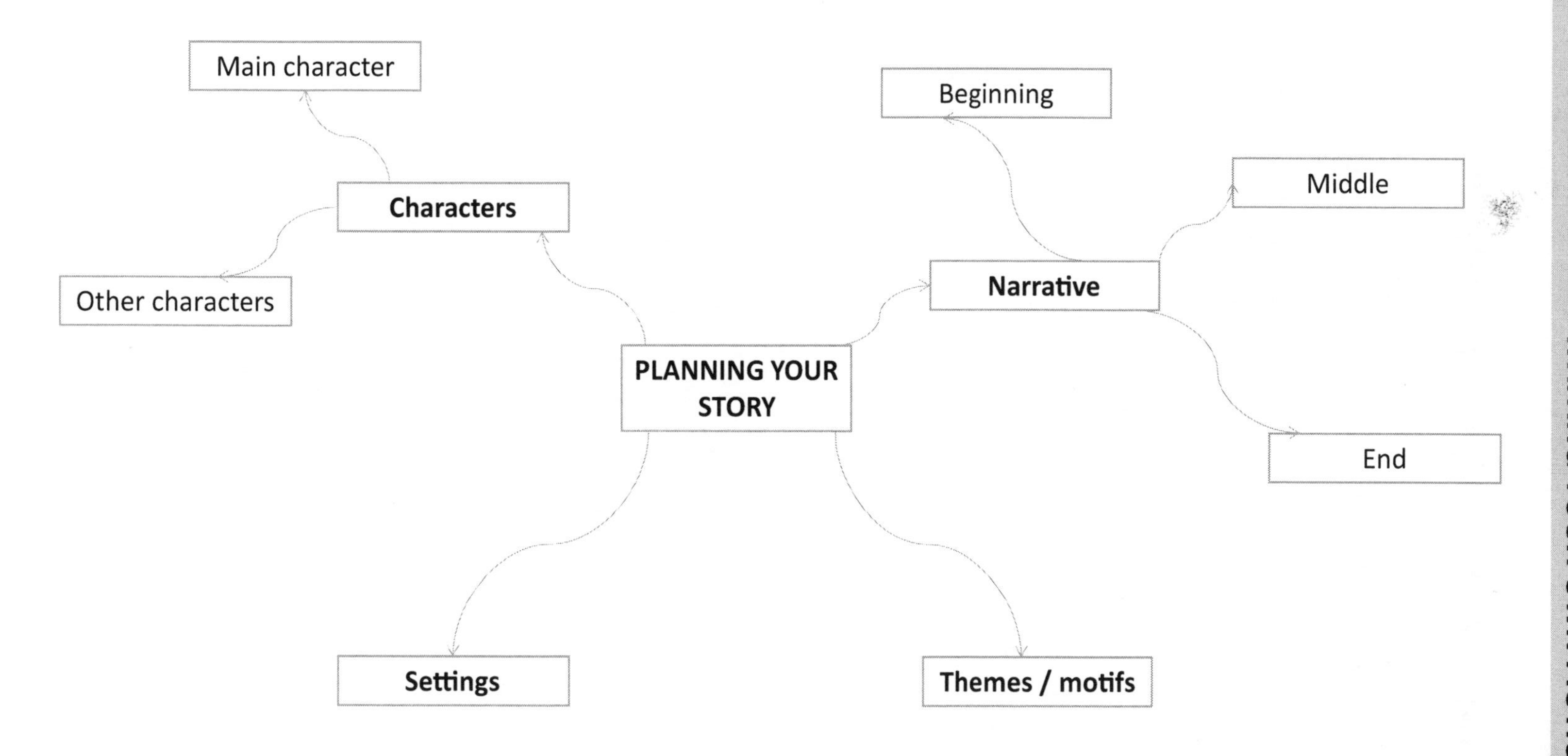
Main character
Characters
Other characters
PLANNING YOUR STORY
Beginning
Middle
Narrative
End
Settings
Themes / motifs

PRACTICE WRITING 1 - 'THE UNKNOWN'

For this story, your title is 'The Unknown'. What you need to do is fill in the boxes below, in order to come up with a plan for a possible narrative.

This is a great way to practice for your reading and comprehension assessment, and improve the key skills required to score highly in your English SATs.

IDEAS

THEMES / MOTIFS

CHARACTERS

SETTINGS

NARRATIVE

PRACTICE WRITING 2 - 'THE PIRATES AND THE HIDDEN TREASURE CHEST'

For this story, your title is 'The Pirates and the Hidden Treasure Chest'. What you need to do is fill in the boxes below, in order to come up with a plan for a possible narrative.

IDEAS

THEMES / MOTIFS

CHARACTERS

SETTINGS

NARRATIVE

TEACHING POETRY

TEACHING POETRY

WHAT IS POETRY?

Poetry is another form of literary writing.

Poems are often written to express feelings, thoughts or ideas. The subject of the poem will depend on what *type* of poem it is.

TYPES OF POETRY

Below is a list of the *types* of poems you will be expected to know for your Key Stage 2 English SATs.

 **Sonnet** Lyrical 14 lines 10 syllables to a line Often about love	 **Narrative** Tells a long story Voice of narrator or character Do not have to rhyme
 **Tanka** Originate in Japan 5 lines Syllable count of 5 / 7 / 5 / 7 / 7 Use of similes, metaphors or personification	 **Limerick** 5 lines Lines 1, 2 and 5 rhyme Lines 3 and 4 rhyme To make you laugh
 **Cinquain** 5 lines 'Cinq' = 5 in French Syllable count of 2 / 4 / 6 / 8 / 2	 **Couplet** 2 lines for a verse Both lines rhyme
 **Haiku** Originate in Japan 3 lines Syllable count of 5 / 7 / 5 Often about nature	 **Acrostic** Word written vertically Each letter starts sentence All lines should relate to the topic of the poem
 **Ode** Ancient Greece Lyric poem Praise of a person or thing Deep feelings or emotions	 **Free Verse** Follows no rules Rhythm, syllables, number of lines, topic = can be anything

TEACHING POETRY

GETTING TO GRIPS WITH POETRY TECHNIQUES

Not only is poetry a form of writing, but it's also a way for poets to express their feelings or ideas through the use of poetry techniques.

I have outlined below the key techniques to consider when creating poetry.

A series of lines that form paragraphs. Each stanza is separated with a line space.

The best way to identify a poem's stanza is to count the number of lines in each paragraph.

2 lines = couplet
3 lines = tercet
4 lines = quantrain
5 lines = cinquain
6 lines = sestet
7 lines = septet
8 lines = octave

The number of lines in a poem will depend on what *type* of poem it is. For example, a haiku poem will usually consist of 3 lines.

A poem will take a particular form. There are many different forms of poetry, and each of which will determine the rhythm, structure and content of the poem.

Lyrical – expressing strong emotions and feelings.

Narrative – telling a story through the use of characters, plotlines, and conversation.

Descriptive – describing the world through the use of elaborate images and adjectives.

TEACHING POETRY

The poet will often express their writing through the use of sound patterns.

Sound patterns are a great way for a reader to understand the rhythm and meaning behind the content of the poem.

- **Rhyme**

The repetition of similar sounding words. This is mostly done with the end words of sentences.

*Looking at the starry **night,***

*The stars and moon that shone so **bright.***

- **Rhythm**

Rhyme and rhythm are NOT the same thing. The rhythm of a poem is the beat you can hear as you read the poem.

The rhythm is created through 'stressed' and 'unstressed' words.

<u>Another way to create sound patterns is the emphasis on groups of words:</u>

- **Alliteration**

Alliteration is the repetition of repeating the same initial in the same line.

***S**mall **S**am **s**wam **s**lowly.*

***L**arge, **l**oud **l**ion.*

- **Onomatopoeia**

These are words that are used that sound like what they are describing.

'bang' *'quack'* *'moo'* *'crash'* *'pow'*

- **Repetition**

The use of repeating a word or phrase. This is done in order to emphasise key themes or ideas.

TEACHING POETRY

One of the biggest things to remember when writing or analysing poetry is the use of language.

Poets will use specific language in order to create meaning.

FIGURATIVE LANGUAGE

Figurative language involves using "figures of speech" that are used to create more of an impact and effect on its reader.

This type of language does NOT have a literal meaning. Instead, it is used to describe someone or something in a way that goes beyond the intended meaning.

There are many ways in which figurative language can be conveyed.

➢ **Similes**

A simile is a figure of speech which compares one thing to another. The reason for this is to make the image more vivid and descriptive.

Most similes use the words "like" or "as".

As busy as a bee.

As cold as ice.

See how the above examples are describing something by comparing it to something else?

➢ **Metaphors**

Metaphors are another figure of speech which uses a word or phrase to describe an object or action, which is not literally appropriate.

Her bedroom is a zoo.

Time is money.

See how the bedroom is being described as a zoo. This could imply that her room is messy. Time is NOT actually money, but this is a way of saying that that you need to put the time in if you wish to make money – time is as valuable as money.

TEACHING POETRY

➢ **Personification**

Personification uses human characteristics to describe inanimate objects – giving objects or 'things' feelings or emotions, or human attributes.

The skies wept.

The flowers were begging for water.

The fact that the skies are weeping, suggests that it is raining.

The flowers were NOT literally begging for water, but this shows how much they needed it.

➢ **Hyperbole**

Hyperboles are exaggerated statements which make something seem more excessive than it actually is.

Your bags weigh a ton!

I am dying of laughter.

These above examples are statements that show exaggeration. The bag doesn't really weigh a literal ton, but is extremely heavy.

The person is not actually dying, but they have been laughing a lot.

➢ **Irony**

Irony is a way of using words or phrases in which the intent of those words actually carries the opposite meaning.

Irony does not always have to be taken negatively. Some poets often use a form of irony that allows the reader to overlook the meaning, and understand different attitudes or conflicting interpretations.

"Oh great! Now you've ruined it!"

You slip on a banana peel, after laughing at someone who slipped on ice.

In the first example, the person doesn't actually mean "great". He is using it to be ironic – he is using it to actually mean the opposite.

In the second example, it is ironic to slip on a banana peel after laughing at someone else who slipped first.

TEACHING POETRY

Are you feeling creative?

Try and come up with a poem of your own for the following titles.

The Snowman
Create a Haiku

The Jungle
Create a Limerick

Sunset
Create a Tanka

Read the poem carefully and answer the following questions.

Poem called *Windy Nights* by Robert Louis Stevenson.

Whenever the moon and stars are set,
Whenever the wind is high,
All night long in the dark and wet,
A man goes riding by.
Law in the night when the fires are out
Why does he gallop and gallop about?

Whenever the trees are crying aloud,
And ships are tossed at sea,
By, on the highway, low and loud,
By at the gallop goes he.
By at the gallop he goes, and then
By he comes back at the gallop again.

Question 1

What type of poem is this? Circle **one**.

Sonnet	Lyrical	Haiku	Ballad

How do you know this?

____

____

Question 2

Line 3 and 4 reads, "All night long in the dark and wet / A man goes riding by". What does the "man" represent?

____

____

Question 3

The poem is a metaphor for which of the following? Tick **one**.

A storm ☐

A horse rider's life ☐

The sea ☐

The darkness of night ☐

Question 4

Why do you think the poet repeats the word "gallop"?

____

____

____

____

Question 5

Write down **two** examples taken from the poem, which describe how the author conveys the idea of a "windy night".

1. ______________________________

2. ______________________________

Read the poems carefully and answer the following questions.

Poems 1 - 4 by How2Become.

POEM 1

There once was a turtle named Joe,
Considered the slowest of the slow.
He entered the race,
With slow as his pace,
On your marks, get set, go!

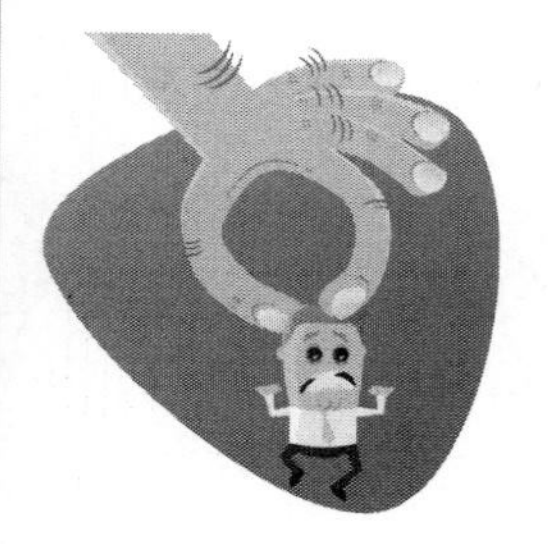

POEM 2

There once was a giant so smelly,
Proud of his overgrown belly.
Feared by all,
Except his friend Paul,
Who told him to cut down on jelly.

POEM 3

There was a boy who loved French bread,
Whose dear mother had often said:
'Cut down or you'll bloat,
Like an oversized goat,
You'll never get out of bed'.

POEM 4

There once was a group of old ladies,
Who roamed around in their Mercedes.
Cheeky as chimps,
With staggering limps,
Following the rules of ol' Hades.

Question 1

What type of poems are poems 1, 2, 3 and 4? Circle **one.**

Haiku	Tanka	Limerick	Sonnet

Give a definition of the poem you have circled.

___

___

Question 2

Which words in Poem 4 are used to rhyme with "Hades"?

__________ and __________

Question 3

Describe how all four of these poems have a similar rhythmic structure. Compare at least **two** poems.

___

___

___

___

Question 4

In Poem 4, the word "ol'" is missing a letter. Which letter do you think is missing? Circle **one**.

Y S D H

Question 5

Using the language and structure of poems 1 to 4, do you think you could use this structure to write about something more serious or sad? Circle **yes** or **no**.

YES **NO**

Explain your answer.

____

____

____

____

____

____

Question 6

There are two similes used in the poems above, rewrite the simile, and state which poem it is from, and why the poet has used that simile.

SIMILE 1

Poem = ______________

Simile = ______________________________________

Why is it used? = ______________________________

____

____

SIMILE 2

Poem = ______________

Simile = ______________________________________

Why is it used? = ______________________________

____

____

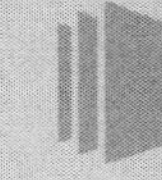

Read the poem carefully and answer the following questions.

Poem called *Summer Time Bliss* by How2Become.

Over the hill tops, the sun so bright
Beautiful brilliant summer light.
A yellow inferno that warmed the air
Walking the countryside without a care.

Butterfly wings that beat up and down
The perfect time for a cotton, white gown.
Singing, dancing, playing hide 'n' seek
The feeling of reaching mountain peak.

Took my hand, summer romance
Now's the time to take a chance.
A world of love; a world of laughter
Something everyone should lust after.

To think of summer is to captivate
The hidden truths and the hidden fate.
What makes this day truly one of a kind
Is the guy who filled my mind.

Down by the river, we lie side-by-side
Glance over to the guy, blue-eyed.
Here he says those special three words
Amongst the breeze, amongst the birds.

Summer time bliss painted with perfection
Vision of rays, heading in one direction.
Follow your heart and follow your dreams
Whether that small, or whether extreme.

Now's the time to say goodbye
All choked up, all starry-eyed.
The perfect day, the perfect bliss
Ended with true love's first kiss.

Question 1

In the 2nd stanza, the poet describes summer as, "The feeling of reaching mountain peak". What do you think the poet means by this?

Question 2

Describe the pattern of the poem and how this ties in with the overall tone of the poem.

Question 3

In the 6th stanza, the poet uses the phrase, "painted with perfection". Explain why the author uses figurative language to draw emphasise on summer and perfection.

Question 4

The term "butterfly" can be used as a symbolic icon for which of the following? Tick **all** that apply.

Vulnerability ☐

Hate ☐

Truth ☐

Loss ☐

Transformation ☐

Beauty ☐

Question 5

The poem is written in which narration? Tick **one**.

1st person	2nd person	3rd person

How can you tell? Give examples of words used in the poem to demonstrate this narration.

____

____

____

____

Question 6

Give **two** quotations from the poem to demonstrate the theme of romance.

EXAMPLE 1

EXAMPLE 2

What impact does this have on the poem and its readers?

Question 7

What can you assume the poet is talking about regarding those "special three words"? How does this tie in with the theme of the poem?

Question 8

How does the poet want you to feel in the last stanza?

Read the poems carefully and answer the following questions.

Poems 5 - 10 by How2Become.

POEM 5

Hoot, alive at night,
Swoops down and preys on dinner.
Keeps watch, golden eyes.

POEM 6

The crazy weather,
Lightning strikes the black, night sky.
Unpredictable.

POEM 7

Four legs, galloping.
My beautiful stallion.
Sitting on his back.

POEM 8

Flashback,
Never forget.
I still hear the voices,
Something unseen but can be heard,
Guess who.

POEM 9

Winter's icy grip,
My fingers as cold as ice.
Building a snow fort,
To escape, to dream, to hope.
Frozen moment, strong silence.

POEM 10

Wind – an angry witch.
Thunder strikes and lights the sky,
Nature's breathing wild.
Trees thrashed and the air whistled,
Like turbulence on a plane.

Question 1

In Poem 5, what animal is the poet talking about? Explain how you know this.

Question 2

Which of the poems is a haiku? Circle **all** of the correct ones.

POEM 5 **POEM 6** **POEM 7** **POEM 8** **POEM 9** **POEM 10**

Question 3

Give a definition of a haiku poem. Use **two** examples from any of the poems to support your answer.

Question 4

In Poem 9, the poet uses the phrase, "winter's icy grip". Is this personification, a simile or a metaphor? Circle your answer.

PERSONIFICATION **SIMILE** **METAPHOR**

Give reasons.

Question 5

Using a pen and a ruler, highlight **ALL** of the similes in **ALL** of the poems.

Question 6

Scarlett loves poetry. In Poem 10, what is the syllable pattern? What *type* of poem is it? Tick **one**.

5 / 7 / 5 / 7 / 7 = Cinquain ☐

5 / 6 / 5 / 7 / 7 = Haiku ☐

7 / 5 / 7 / 5 / 5 = Cinquain ☐

5 / 7 / 7 / 5 / 7 = Tanka ☐

5 / 7 / 5 / 7 / 7 = Tanka ☐

Question 7

How does the author convey the idea of isolation in Poem 9?

____

____

____

____

Question 8

Poet 10 uses the term “thrashed”. What does this mean?

____

____

____

____

Question 9

How many syllables are there in the first and last line of a cinquain? Circle **one**.

5 7 4 6 2

Question 10

In Poem 8, explain how you know the poet is talking about personal experiences.

____

____

____

____

Question 11

Explain why Poem 10 compares an "angry witch" to the weather. What does this symbolise?

____

____

____

____

Question 12

Another word for "stallion", is...

Bird	Donkey	Horse	Dog

Question 13

Two of the poets use alliteration in their writing. Which **two** poets use alliteration? Write the alliterated words below.

POET = ____________________

ALLITERATION = ____________________

POET = ____________________

ALLITERATION = ____________________

ANSWERS TO TEACHING POETRY

Windy Nights

Q1. Lyrical

Lyrical poems are poems that are expressed musically. In other words, you can imagine singing along to them.

Q2. The man is representing a horse rider.

Q3. A horse rider's life

Q4. The poet repeats the word "gallop" because it allows the reader to visualise a horse, which is relevant to the storyline, because the man is a horse rider. Also, the repetition of the word helps with the rhythm of the overall poem – which is made to sound like horses hooves hitting the ground.

Q5. (1) "Whenever the trees are crying aloud". This links to the title of the poem, "Windy Nights", as it suggests that the trees are making noises from the wind.

(2) "And ships are tossed at sea". This demonstrates that the sea is rough and therefore reinforces the notion of wind.

Poems 1 – 4

Q1. Limerick

A limerick is a poem that uses rhythm and rhyming patterns with the intention to be funny and/or silly.

Q2. Mercedes and ladies

Q3. In all of the poems, they all follow the same rhythmic structure. The last word of the first, second and last line rhyme. The third and fourth line rhyme. For example, in Poem 1, lines 1, 2 and 5 end with the words "Joe", "slow" and "go". Lines 3 and 4 end with the words "race" and "pace". In Poem 3, lines 1, 2 and 5 end with the words "bread", "said" and "bed". Lines 3 and 4 end with the words "bloat" and "gloat".

Q4. D

Q5. *This answer is based on personal preference, you just need to provide solid reasoning for your choice.*

(For example, you could circle "no" because the structure and style of these poems are used to be upbeat, funny and silly. The tone of these poems is very laid back and therefore could not be used to talk about something more serious.)

Q6. "Like an oversized goat" (poem 3). The poet has used this simile not only for humorous effect, but also to emphasise that the boy's overeating mirrors that of an engorged animal.

"Cheeky as chimps" (poem 4). The poet uses this simile to suggest that the old ladies are lively, immature and bold – the same characteristics as a chimp.

Summer Time Bliss

Q1. The poet describes summer as being like, "the feeling of reaching mountain peak". This could suggest that it is extremely hot (the temperature has reached its peak). Or, this statement could suggest the excitement and happiness you get from reaching your goals (in this case, it would be the happiness of summer time beginning).

Q2. The pattern of the poem contains 7 stanzas, each of which are 4 lines long. Each stanza follows the same rhythmic pattern, by which the first and second line rhyme, and the third and fourth line rhyme. This creates an upbeat rhythm, and this positivity is great for a poem on summer time, love and happiness.

Q3. The use of the poet's figurative language, "painted with perfection", demonstrates the idealistic and perfected style which can be achieved from a painting. This is compared to the positive attributes that summer brings. The feelings that are related to summer time are described as "painted", and this metaphor is used to highlight the sheer bliss, precision and beauty in which both paintings and summer have.

Q4. Vulnerability, truth, transformation and beauty

Q5. 1st person

The poem is written in first person. This is demonstrated through the poet referring to themselves. The use of the words "my mind", "my hand" and "we lie" illustrate first person tense. The poet has used first person narration as it provides the reader with a more personal account of events, which makes it easier for readers to empathise with the poet and visualise the scene.

Q6. "What makes this day truly one of a kind"

"Ended with true love's first kiss".

The poet recalls on their memory to highlight how summer was related to these particular memories. The poet can look back on their summer with memories full of love and admiration. This draws the reader in by creating a sense of summer romance and perfection.

Q7. I love you

You can assume that when the poet talks about those "special three words", these words are 'I love you'. This can be inferred based on the overall context of the poem. The whole poem is based on love and romance, and therefore these words seem fitting with the rest of the poem.

Q8. The poet uses the last stanza to draw on a close of summer romance. Although the memory of a true loves kiss remains, the fact that they are saying goodbye, allows the reader to feel sadness. However, the poet still finishes the poem in a happy way, and therefore the reader should still be feeling a sense of romance and happiness.

Poems 5 – 10

Q1. In Poem 5, the poet is talking about an owl. We know this because the language in the poem shows characteristics of an owl. For example, the use of the word "hoot" is the sound an owl makes. "Alive at night" indicates it is an animal that is awake during the night. "Keeps watch, golden eyes" is describing the look of an owl, which has huge, golden eyes.

Q2. Poem 5, Poem 6, Poem 7

Q3. A haiku is a type of Japanese poem, which uses 3 lines. The syllable pattern of a haiku is 5 / 7 / 5. For example, the first line should have five syllables ("Hoot, alive at night"). The second line should have seven syllables ("Lightning strikes the black, night sky"). And finally, the third line should have five syllables ("Sitting on his back").

Q4. Personification

The phrase "winter's icy grip" is describing the coldness of winter, by giving it human characteristics (by gripping on). This therefore is an example of personification.

Q5. The words or phrases that you should have highlighted are as follows:

- As cold as ice
- Like turbulence on a plane

Q6. 5 / 7 / 5 / 7 / 7 = Tanka

Q7. The poet conveys the idea of isolation through the use of the "snow fort". The snow fort acts as a symbol for isolation because it is a way of escaping the outside world, and entering a place of solitude and loneliness. The poet also implies, "To escape, to dream, to hope" which reinforces what the snow fort stands for. The snow fort is a way of isolating yourself so you can visualise what you want in the future. It is a way of escaping.

Q8. The term "thrashed", in context of the passage, is used to describe something moving in a violent and compulsive way. For example, the poet describes the trees as thrashing, which implies that they are being blown in all different directions by the wind.

Q9. 2

Remember, in a cinquain the syllable pattern is 2 / 4 / 6 / 8 / 2.

Q10. In poem 8, the poet is talking about personal experiences, because he uses the word "I". Also, the use of the term "flashback" suggests personal memories.

Q11. Poem 10 compares an "angry witch" to the weather, because it allows the reader to visualise fierce and unpredictable characteristics – much like the weather being described in the poem. The poet describes the weather as being fierce, and this is how a witch is often portrayed.

Q12. Horse

Q13. Poem 5 = "strong silence"

Poem 10 = "trees thrashed"

HOW ARE YOU GETTING ON?

UNDERSTANDING NON-FICTION TEXTS

UNDERSTANDING NON-FICTION TEXTS

WHAT IS NON-FICTION?

You need to know the difference between fiction and non-fiction.

Opposite to fiction, **non-fiction** is writing based on facts and real-life events. This provides readers with information that should be taken as factual and accurate.

TYPES OF NON-FICTION

There are many different *types* of texts that are non-fiction. Each text is written to serve a particular purpose.

NON-FICTION (INSTRUCTION TEXTS)

PURPOSE OF THE TEXT	FEATURES	EXAMPLES
• Instruction texts tell you how to do or make something.	• Step-by-step instructions. • Headers and sub-headings.	• Cookery books. • Instruction manuals.

NON-FICTION (EXPLANATION TEXTS)

PURPOSE OF THE TEXT	FEATURES	EXAMPLES
• Explanation texts provide information on how something happens. • They also discuss why things happen.	• Technical language. • Specific knowledge on a topic. • Diagrams and images that help show what is being spoken about. • Explain processes and effects.	• Life cycles. • Explaining how something works, like a volcano.

NON-FICTION (PERSUASIVE TEXTS)

PURPOSE OF THE TEXT	FEATURES	EXAMPLES
• To try and get your reader to believe a particular view point. • Often based on one point of view. • To inform, to change their minds or encourage them to do something.	• Strong, persuasive language. • Good use of adjectives. • Emotive language. • Repetition.	• Adverts. • Brochures. • TV advertising. • Posters. • Leaflets. • Billboards.

UNDERSTANDING NON-FICTION TEXTS

NON-FICTION (DISCUSSION TEXTS)

PURPOSE OF THE TEXT	FEATURES	EXAMPLES
• A text that offers alternative points of view. • Discussing an issue or general topic.	• For and against arguments. • Use of emotive language. • The conclusion usually takes one side for either for or against.	• Newspaper articles. • Reviews (book, film, theatre). • Debates.

NON-FICTION (RECOUNT TEXTS)

PURPOSE OF THE TEXT	FEATURES	EXAMPLES
• Recollection of events. • Retelling something that has already happened.	• Introduction and conclusion. • Usually in chronological order.	• Journals. • Diaries. • Write-ups of experiments.

NON-FICTION (NON-CHRONOLOGICAL TEXTS)

PURPOSE OF THE TEXT	FEATURES	EXAMPLES
• To keep a record of information about a specific topic.	• Uses technical language. • Diagrams, photos and illustrations. • Contains factual information about the topic. • Opening statement and conclusion.	• Specific books based on particular subjects. • Encyclopaedias. • Catalogue. • Letter.

All non-fiction texts can be placed into one of the above categories. Some non-fiction texts can be placed in more than one of the above categories, and therefore serve multiple purposes.

REMEMBER

Each non-fiction text can be placed under a sub-heading:

Recount, non-chronological, discussion, persuasion, explanation and *instruction.*

UNDERSTANDING NON-FICTION TEXTS

THE USE OF LANGUAGE

Language is a key component when it comes to writing any literary text. The language used in a text will depend on what *type* of non-fiction text it is.

For example:

- A leaflet will use very different language than an extract from a diary. Both are examples of non-fiction texts, but they are both written for a different purpose:
    - A leaflet will often contain facts and use emotional language in order to emphasise a particular point of view.
    - A diary extract is an informal piece of writing which is written from personal experience. This can use informal language such as slang.

What language would be used to write about a science experiment?

What language would be used in an advert for banning smoking?

What language would be used to write a newspaper article?

UNDERSTANDING NON-FICTION TEXTS

PRESENTATION AND STRUCTURE

In non-fiction texts, not only is language an important factor, but the way it is structured and presented also has an impact on the readers.

The structure

The structure of a text refers to how the text is laid out:

- *Does the text use paragraphs?*
- *Does the text have an introduction and conclusion?*
- *Is it in chronological order?*
- *It is formal or informal?*
- *What does the author want you to feel after reading the text?*

The structure will depend on what *kind* of text it is.

If it's a report, you will often see an introduction, explanation of findings and analysis, and a conclusion.

If it's a recipe, you will be given step-by-step instructions on how to complete each step of the process, and this will sometimes use diagrams to demonstrate the explanation.

Look out for the key features and structure of a text. This will help you to identify what *type* of text you are reading.

The presentation

The presentation of a non-fiction text is how it is presented to the reader.

For example, a newspaper article is instantly recognisable because it is laid out in columns. An advert will often contain a large image and few words in order to put the point across quickly.

The presentation of a text helps the reader identify what kind of message is going to be portrayed.

UNDERSTANDING NON-FICTION TEXTS

ANALYSING THE TEXT

In order to score highly on the English Comprehension section of your SATs, you will need to be able to analyse the information you are given.

When you are reading through a text, it can seem a bit scary and overwhelming because there is so much to take in. You need to take in the information that is **relevant** to the question.

You will need to read the text thoroughly and then pick out the key bits of information you can use.

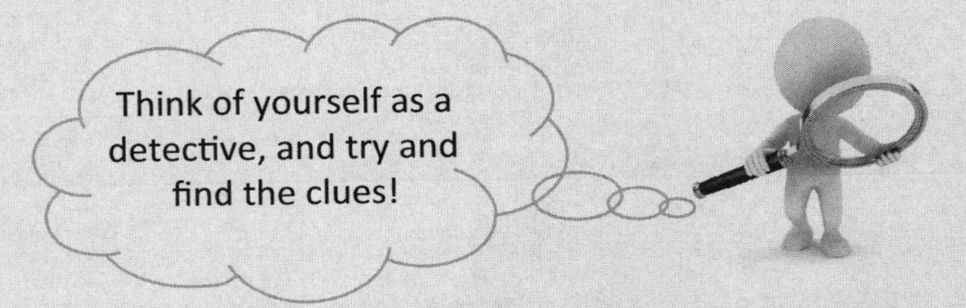

Remember = some questions will specifically ask you to find evidence from the passage. This is where you need to quote from the passage. Some questions carry more marks, and these questions will often need longer answers, which means you need to add more detail.

KNOWING FACTS FROM OPINIONS

Another key thing you need to be able to do, is know when something is fact, or whether it is an opinion.

- **Facts** are statements that are the truth. Nobody can argue with a fact.
  - o *Paris is the capital city of France = FACT*
- **Opinions** are statements of what people believe.
  - o *Paris is the most beautiful city in the word = OPINION*

Just because the text offers an opinion, it doesn't mean to say that you think the same thing. You might have an alternative opinion on something, and therefore you could argue against the text.

If you offer an opinion, you need to make sure that you support your answer with reasoning. You need to justify your argument, by saying why you disagree with the reader, or offer other reasons as to why you think you're right.

UNDERSTANDING NON-FICTION TEXTS

USING EVIDENCE

In order for your answers to be strong, you need to make sure that you support your answers using evidence from the text.

<u>You can do this in two ways:</u>

1. Take a direct quote from the text and explain what it means.
2. Paraphrase what the author has said in the text and explain what it means.

By using evidence from the text, not only are you showing that you have read the text correctly and are able to pinpoint certain information, but it will guarantee you top marks!

INTERPRETING THE TEXT

Another skill that is required for English Comprehension, is the ability to read the text and interpret the information and messages being put across.

Sometimes you will be given long written texts, of which you will need to break down and understand what the main points are. This requires you to **summarise** what has been said. You should be able to summarise a passage in 2 or 3 lines.

IMPACTING THE READER

A non-fiction text is mainly written with the intention of creating a certain impact on their reader or audience.

The text needs to be informative, persuasive and straight to the point in order to create a huge impact on its targeted audience / reader.

It is important that you know who your audience or reader are going to be. That way you can use the correct language and techniques to put your message across.

For example, there is no point using informal language in a document that is highly technical. It would be pointless to use scientific language in a TV advert for young children because they simply won't understand.

Read the text carefully and answer the following questions.

Discovering Dinosaurs by How2Become.

VELOCIRAPTOR

From the cretaceous period, the Velociraptor was a speedy dinosaur, reaching up to 40 mph. This made it easy for them to capture their prey. This type of dinosaur was meat-eating, and used their sharp claws to tear away the meat from its prey. Generally, the dinosaur would feast on plant-eating dinosaurs such as protoceratops and other herbivores.

This dinosaur was 6 feet in length, 2 feet in height and weighed approximately 25 kilograms.

They had an S curve in their necks and had really thin legs. They stood on their hind legs and were able to jump great distances.

Velociraptors were considered highly intelligent. They would often travel in packs, and were able to close in their prey. This fearsome predator's name means "quick plunder".

BRACHIOSAURUS

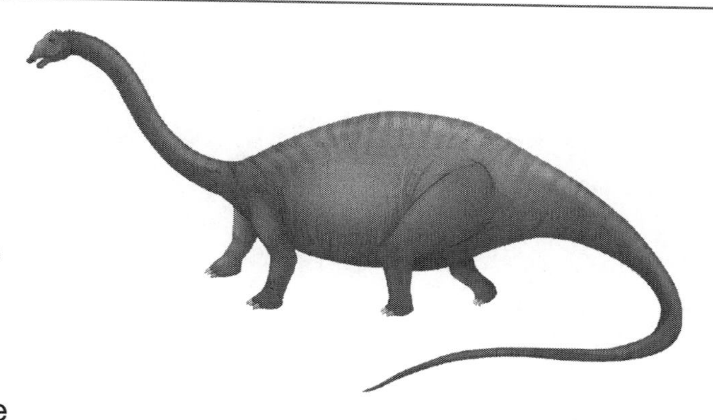

One of the least intelligent dinosaurs, the Brachiosaurus was the largest and heaviest dinosaur that lived in the Jurassic Period.

These dinosaurs walked on all four legs, and were estimated to weigh between 30 and 45 tons. They were herbivores that only ate foliage that was high above the ground, and were said to consume between 200 and 400 kilograms of food per day.

They had extremely long necks to reach food. Their front legs were longer than their back legs, which meant that they were unable to rear up on their back legs.

Scientists believed that the Brachiosaurus was a warm-blooded dinosaur, like mammals.

TYRANNOSAURUS REX

The T-Rex was one of the biggest meat eating dinosaurs. This carnivorous dinosaur had a large brain, which allowed them to be intelligent when it came to finding their prey.

These dinosaurs lived in the late Cretaceous Period and were renowned for using their exceptional vision and smell to hunt down other animals.

It had small arms which only had two fingers. Their teeth were razor sharp and were about 8 inches long. They had a flexible neck which allowed them to attack in all directions. Their tail was used to help with their balance, and their powerful legs allowed them to be strong and speedy.

TRICERATOPS

The name Triceratops can be broken down into two – 'tri' meaning three, and 'ceratops' meaning horned face.

These dinosaurs lived in the late Cretaceous Period. It required its three horns in order to protect themselves from predators. These herbivores were about 8 metres in length and 3 metres in height. The skull of a Triceratops could grow to an astonishing 2 metres in length.

The dinosaur had strong stubby legs to support their heavy bodies. They had a sharp, parrot-like beak and a bony frill which acted as a guard to support their necks.

Question 1

What type of text is this? How do you know?

Question 2

Which dinosaur/s belonged to the Cretaceous Period? Circle **all** that apply.

TRICERATOPS **T-REX** **BRACHIOSAURUS** **VELOCIRAPTOR**

Question 3

What does 'Triceratops' mean? How does this dinosaur use this to their advantage?

Question 4

If dinosaurs still existed, which dinosaur would you fear the most? Explain your answer.

Question 5

How do you think dinosaurs became extinct? Use your own knowledge, or be creative!

Question 6

Preston asks: Which dinosaur used their necks to help them feast? Tick **one**.

T-Rex ☐

Triceratops ☐

Velociraptor ☐

Brachiosaurus ☐

Question 7

Scientists believed that that the Brachiosaurus was a warm blooded dinosaur. Explain how this could be disputed.

Read the text carefully and answer the following questions.

Superhero Showdown by How2Become.

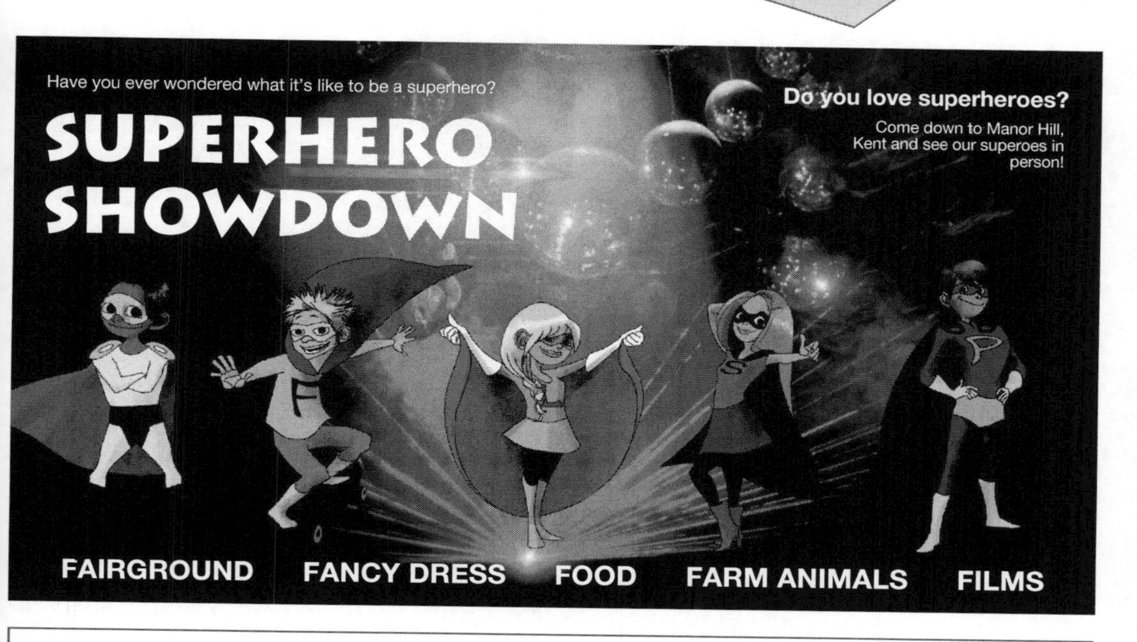

FACT SHEET

Introducing our fun-loving superheroes:

Anil **Freddie** **Lalita** **Scarlett** **Preston**

DATE
18th August 2016

TIME
15:00

VENUE
Manor Hill, Kent

PRICE
Adult ticket (over 18) = £5.00
Children (5 and under) = FREE
Children (over 5) = £2.10
Concessions = £2.10
Family (2 adults, 2 children) = £7.00

Question 1

What type of non-fiction text is this? Tick **one**.

Recount text ☐

Persuasive text ☐

Discussion text ☐

Explanation text ☐

Question 2

Using your answer to part 1, explain why you think it is that type of non-fiction text.

____

____

____

____

____

____

Question 3

Does the text make you want to attend the Superhero Showdown? Explain your answer.

____

____

____

____

____

____

Question 4

What type of technique is the 5 Fs (Fairground, Fancy dress, Food, Farm animals, Films)? Circle **one** answer.

Repetition **Alliteration** **Bathos** **Allegory**

Question 5

Using your answer to question 4, explain why the author has used this literary technique in their text.

Question 6

Why do you think the author has used the phrase, "Have you ever wondered what it's like to be a superhero?" How does this appeal to the reader/audience?

Question 7

Using the information above, 3 adults, 2 children (under the age of 5) and 3 children (over the age of 5) wish to attend the Showdown. Work out the total cost to get into the Superhero Showdown (without using a family ticket).

Read the text carefully and answer the following questions.

Understanding 'The Green Cross Code' by How2Become.

Every child needs to understand the importance of road safety. Here is an outline of *The Green Cross Code*. Remember, this can save a life!

1. First of all, you should find a safe place to cross.
Try and use zebra, puffin, pelican or toucan crossings where possible. Does the road have a footbridge you can go over? Does the road have islands which you can wait on? Is the road controlled by school crossing patrol?

If none of these are available to you, find a place where you can see every direction. Make sure you are visible by standing in a place where you're not hidden. Even wearing bright or florescent clothing will help you to be seen.

Don't stand behind parked cars, or on corners. This is not a safe place to cross.

2. Make sure you are a good distance away from the kerb.
Don't stand too close to the kerb when looking to see whether or not it is safe to cross. A vehicle (or cyclist) might be driving too close to the kerb and this will likely cause an accident.

Make sure you stand back from the kerb and have a good look in both directions. Remember to look more than once!

3. Look and listen!
Look both ways. Look more than once. Look for hazards. Listen for any oncoming traffic. Just because you can't see something, doesn't mean there is nothing there. You might be able to hear something in the distance.

4. Don't rush – if traffic is coming, wait!
Keep looking in both directions. Do not rush to get across. Wait until you see a safe gap between the traffic. You need to make sure there is enough time to reach the other side of the road. Just because traffic isn't close, doesn't mean it is safe – they might be travelling at a fast speed.

5. When it's safe, proceed to the other side.
Don't run, walk! Keep looking as you cross the road, just in case something comes out of nowhere. Look out for cyclists and motorbikes. Walk straight to the other side, don't walk diagonally.

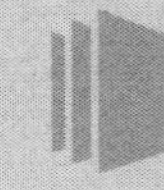

Question 1

Why do you think you are advised NOT to cross diagonally?

____

____

Question 2

From the passage, which two places are listed as places that you should NOT use to cross a road?

____________________ and ____________________

Question 3

List the four types of crossings that are mentioned in the passage.

1. ____________________

2. ____________________

3. ____________________

4. ____________________

Question 4

What kind of non-fiction text is *Understanding the Green Cross Code?* Circle one.

PERSUASIVE **EXPLANATION** **INSTRUCTION** **DISCUSSION**

Question 5

Using your answer to the above question, how do you know this?

Question 6

Why is it important not to stand too close to the kerb when looking for traffic?

Question 7

Which sense, out of the following, are you told to use first? Circle **one**.

SOUND **TASTE** **SIGHT** **SMELL** **TOUCH**

Question 8

From your understanding and using an example, what is the definition of a "hazard"?

Question 9

How does the writer tell you to make yourself more visible to traffic? Write **two** different statements.

1. ____

____

2. ____

____

Question 10

Why do you think *The Green Cross Code* is named as it is?

____

____

____

Read the text carefully and answer the following questions.

Global Warming by How2Become.

Global warming is already having an impact on our community, and without taking action, the issue will continue to become more of a concern and will impact the future of our world.

Climate change doesn't just mean that the weather will get somewhat warmer; this is not always the case. As the planet begins to heat, climate patterns will fluctuate and this will result in extreme and unpredictable weather conditions. This means that across the world, some weather conditions may be extremely hot, whilst others will experience torrential rain or plummeting temperatures. These are a direct consequence of the way in which the planet has been treated.

In many ways, climate change is simply a result of human action. Burning fossil fuels is a clear example of how, over the past 15 decades, the world has become more industrialised and changed the balance of the carbon cycle. Burning fossil fuels such as oil, gas and coal converts carbon into carbon dioxide, and unless it is captured, the carbon dioxide is released into the atmosphere. This climate change is characterised by higher than average global temperatures and the increase in sea levels.

Not only does burning fossil fuels contribute to global warming, but breeding cattle is another contributing factor. Within our industrialised society, nations have bred vast numbers of methane-producing animal stock. A moose, for example, contributes massively to global warming – expelling enough methane to represent approximately 2,100kg of carbon dioxide emissions, similar to the impact of driving for 8,000 miles.

Forests also have a huge role to play in fighting climate change. They can be used to absorb and store carbon in their soil and trees. Yet, we continue to cut these forests down with no hindsight of the consequences that follow. Why? Why do we continue these actions if we know what the outcome and consequences are going to be? If these forests are frequently being cut down, then all the stored emissions from the trees will be released into the atmosphere. Up to one fifth of greenhouse gas emissions comes from deforestation and forest degradation, which indicates the scale of the issue and the impact it causes in terms of global warming.

Question 1

In the second paragraph, the author uses the term "fluctuate". Based on the context of the passage, what do you think this means?

____

____

____

____

____

____

Question 2

Give **three** consequences of the climate changing.

1. ____

____

2. ____

____

3. ____

____

Question 3

What **two** factors are listed in the passage as contributing to global warming?

1. ____

____

2. ____

____

Question 4

In the last paragraph, the author often refers to 'we' as a society. Why do you think the author has done this in this particular text?

Question 5

How much greenhouse gas is emitted from deforestation? Circle **one**.

ONE THIRD **HALF** **ONE QUARTER** **ONE FIFTH**

Question 6

For the following statements, put a **tick** or **cross** to say whether each statement is **true** or **false**.

Statement	
Global warming is a result of man.	
Global warming will see all temperatures rise.	
Deforestation plays no role in global warming.	
Burning fossil fuels is a contributing factor to global warming.	
Moose expel methane which produces carbon dioxide.	

Read the text carefully and answer the following questions.

Unexplained Object in British Skies by How2Become.

UNEXPLAINED OBJECT IN BRITISH SKIES

A BIZARRE, UNIDENTIFIED object was once again reported soaring the skies right here in Britain.

Two reports were made on the very same day and were claimed to have happened just minutes apart. Paranormal experts and scientific investigators are staggered by this profound event, and are furthering their inquiries.

The first incident was reported at 08:16am on Wednesday, and the unnamed witness claims to have been "fetching her daily newspaper" when the extraordinary thing happened. She claims that she's "never seen anything like it" and "had to look twice".

A flying object, which was described by both witnesses as being triangular-shaped, was caught flying through the skies over the countryside in Lenham, Kent.

The next reporting was at 09:32am, 2,000 miles south from the first location.

Sammie Harris, 26, and her husband, Daniel, 29, were driving back to their house, when they both looked out the passenger-side window. Sammie pulled over the car, and they both stepped out.

"It was a flat object, a light colour, which drifted through the air. Like a shooting star falling from the sky, the object appeared to be heading downwards", Daniel claimed, with both nerves and excitement in his voice.

"If my husband had not been there, I don't think anyone would have believed me". Sammie was unsure what she saw at first, and when she pointed it out to Daniel, they both came to the same conclusion.

All of the witnesses described the object as having a slight yellow tinge to it, which flashed in time with a regular heartbeat.

Neither of the witnesses were able to film nor capture the event on camera.

Question 1

What type of example is this non-fiction text? How do you know?

Question 2

From just reading the heading 'Unexplained Object in British Skies', what can you assume the story will be about?

Question 3

What was the name of the first witness? Tick **one**.

Sammie Harris ☐

Daniel ☐

Unknown ☐

Lenny ☐

Find a quote from the passage to support your answer.

Question 4

Do you think this piece of text is reliable? Explain your answer using evidence from the text.

____

____

____

____

____

____

Question 5

When was the incident reported first?

____

Question 6

How is the "object" described? Use three examples from the passage.

1. ____

____

2. ____

____

3. ____

____

Question 7

In the first paragraph, the author uses the word "soaring". Write two **alternative** words which mean the same thing (synonyms).

____________________ and ____________________

Question 8

What does the author compare the flashing lights of the object to?

____

____

Question 9

How many miles apart were both sightings of the flying object? Circle **one**.

1000 miles **1000 kilometres** **2000 kilometres** **2000 miles**

Question 10

The author uses a simile in this article. Quote this simile.

____

Read the text carefully and answer the following questions.

The Human Body by How2Become.

THE HUMAN BODY

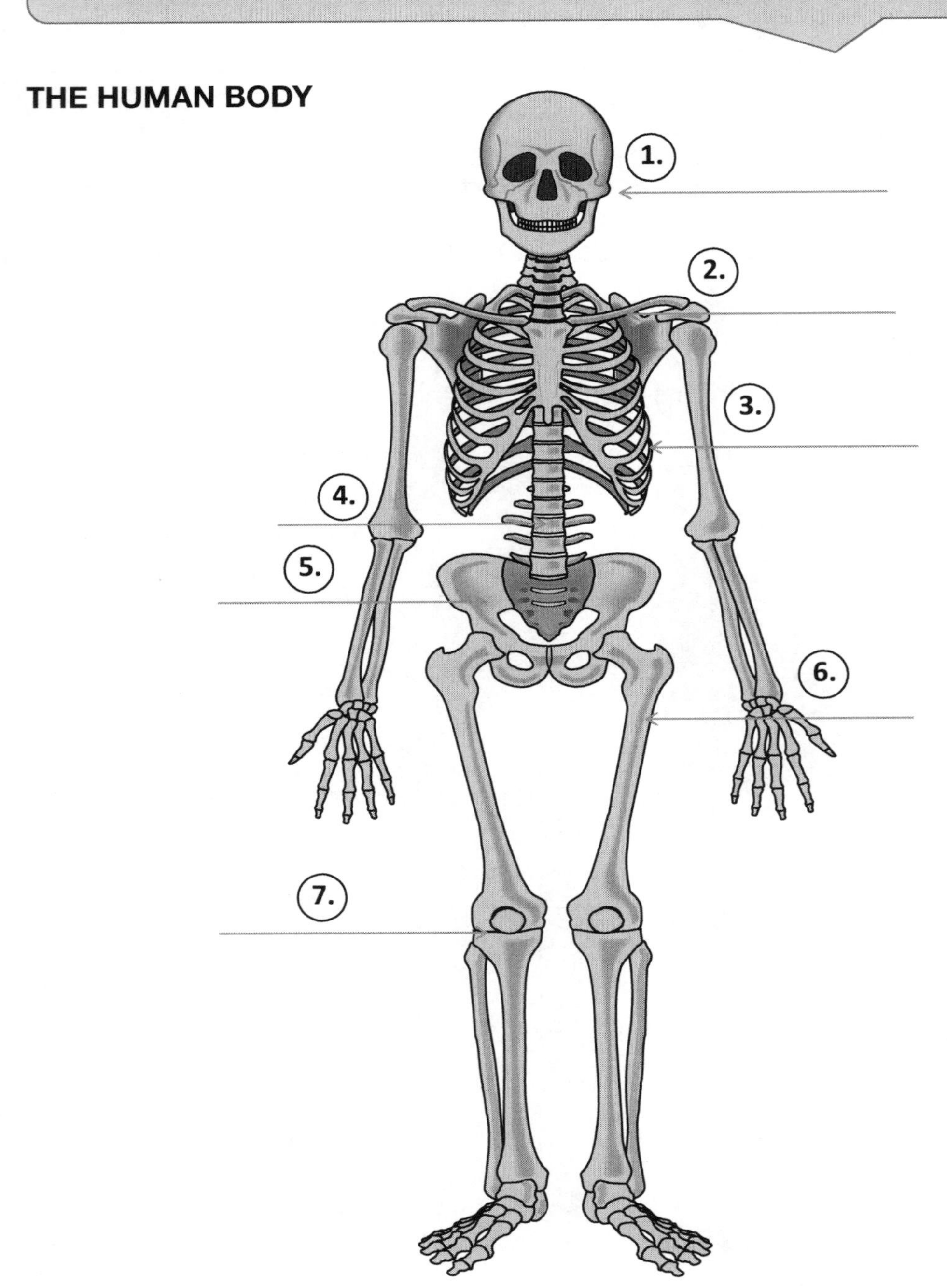

FACT SHEET

The human body is made up of lots of different bones. Our bones grow as we get bigger.

The Human Skeleton

Skull – The skull protects our brain.

Rib cage – Our rib cage protects our lungs and heart. They also help to protect major blood vessels in the upper body.

Spine/backbone – Our spine allows us to stand up straight and gives us posture. It also protects the spinal nerve.

Pelvis – The pelvis supports our legs, our spine, our abdomen and the lower back. This also provides us with a strong posture.

Animal Skeletons

The majority of animals also have a skeleton to help support and protect their bodies. Animals including horses, whales, dogs and mice all have a skeleton.

Some animals have their skeleton on the outside of their body, like lobsters, crabs and other insects. They are known as **exoskeletons**.

Some animals such as jellyfish, worms and snails do not have a skeleton.

How Skeletons Move

The skeleton works by the bones being supported by **joints**. Joints are where two bones join together. These joints allows us to bend. Kneecaps, ankles and wrists are all examples of bone joints.

Muscles are attached to our bones with tendons. They work in pairs and stretch out, which allows us to be mobile. When one of the muscles contracts, the other relaxes. The **heart** is the most important muscle in the body.

Question 1

Label the diagram of The Human Body.

Question 2

The skeleton does three main jobs. What are they?

1. ______________________________

____

2. ______________________________

____

3. ______________________________

____

Question 3

Give two examples, from the fact sheet, of animals that do not have a skeleton.

1. ______________________________

____

2. ______________________________

____

Question 4

Describe the function of joints, using an example of a body joint and explain how it works.

____

____

____

____

____

Question 5

Explain the functionality of our spine.

____

____

Question 6

What organs are protected by our rib cage? Circle **two**.

BRAIN **HEART** **ABDOMEN** **LIVER** **LUNGS**

Question 7

Put a **tick** or **cross** in the boxes below, based on whether the statement is **true** or **false**.

All animals have a skeleton. ☐

Muscles are attached to bones using tendons. ☐

The lungs are the most important muscle in the body. ☐

Our bones grow as we grow. ☐

Horses have a backbone. ☐

Only one muscle is needed in order to contract. ☐

Based on the information, an elbow is a bone joint. ☐

Read the text carefully and answer the following questions.

The Water Cycle by How2Become.

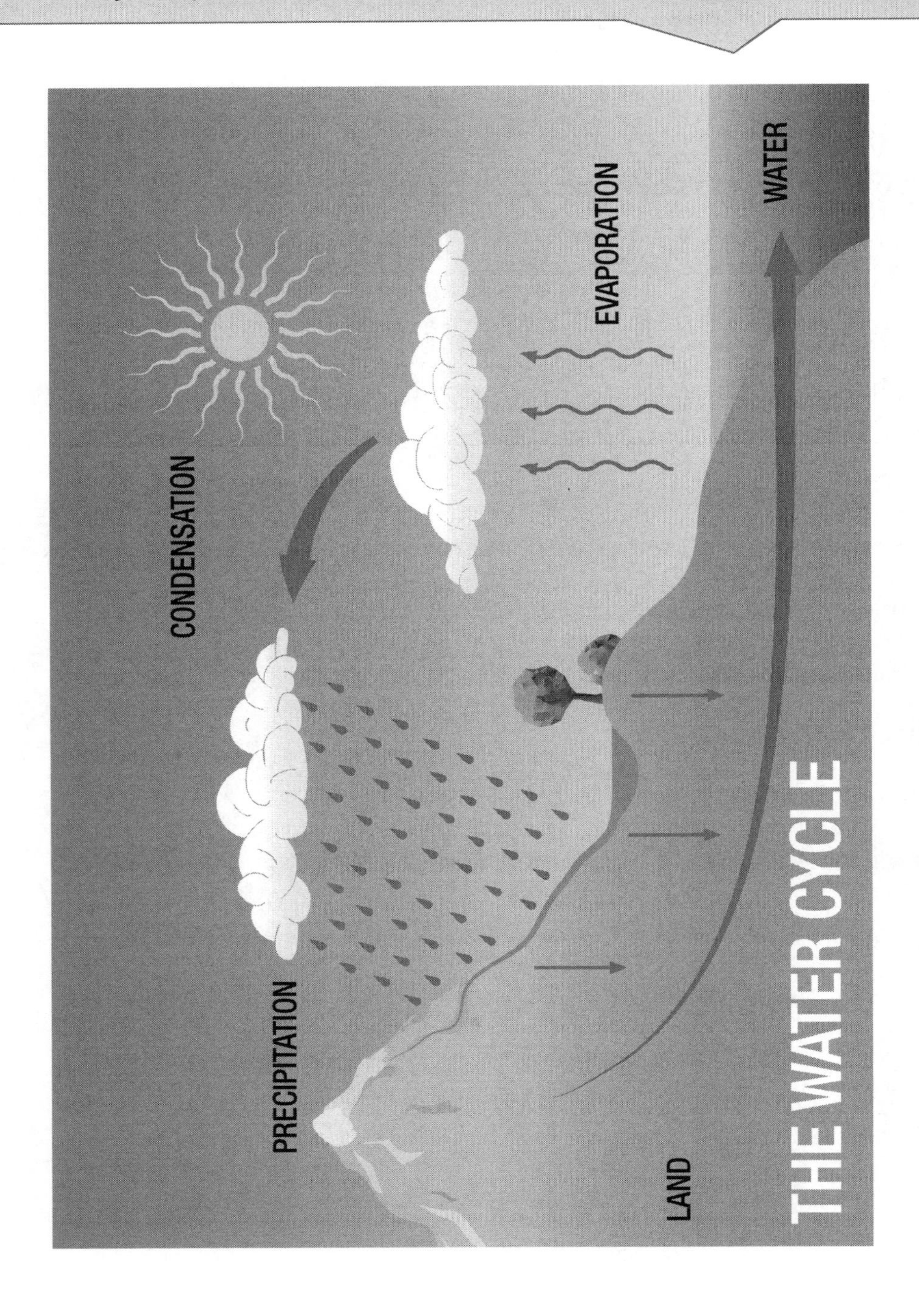

THE WATER CYCLE – PROCESS

On earth, water is constantly being **recycled**. The water we use is in a life cycle process, and this process is known as **the water cycle**.

STEP 1

Water gets evaporated from the earth, into the air.

- The sun heats up the water and causes it to turn from a liquid formation to water vapour. You cannot see the water rising from the ground into the air.
- Water is evaporated from rainwater on the ground, as well as from lakes, rivers and ponds.

STEP 2

The water vapour condenses and forms clouds.

- After the water is in the air, the water vapour cools down and turns into tiny water droplets. These droplets form a cloud.

STEP 3

Rain begins to fall.

- Clouds become heavy, and these tiny water droplets fall back to earth. This is either in the form of rain, sleet or snow.

STEP 4

Water returns to the sea.

- Rain water lays on the ground and is collected in lakes and rivers, and transports it back to the sea. The process starts all over again.

Question 1

When water gets evaporated, it turns into what? Circle **one**.

RAIN **SNOW** **WATER VAPOUR** **STEAM**

Question 2

From the text, how would you define the word "recycled"?

____

____

____

Question 3

The process of water vapour turning into clouds is called what?

____

Question 4

What type of non-fiction text is this? Tick **one**.

Instruction text ☐

Persuasive text ☐

Discussion text ☐

Explanation text ☐

How do you know this?

____

____

Question 5

How are clouds formed?

Question 6

In your own words, explain the water cycle.

Question 7

If there was a lack of rainfall, how do you think this would affect the water cycle? Use examples from the text to support your answer.

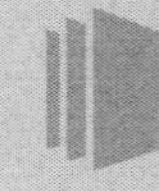

ANSWERS TO UNDERSTANDING NON-FICTION TEXTS

Discovering Dinosaurs

Q1. Non-chronological report. This type of non-fiction documents information about a specific topic (in this case, the subject being dinosaurs). The use of photos and facts allows the reader to know what type of text they are reading, because it offers a series of facts and illustrations to talk about a certain subject.

Q2. Velociraptor, T-Rex and Triceratops

Q3. The name 'Triceratops' can be broken down into two parts. 'Tri' means three. 'Ceratops' means horn faced. Therefore this type of dinosaur was known for their three horns on their head. This type of dinosaur used its three horns as a way of protecting themselves from predators.

Q4. *This answer is based on personal thought. You can choose any answer so long as you support your answer with evidence from the text*

(For example, you may fear the T-Rex the most because it is one of the biggest meat-eating dinosaurs. This means that it would kill you for food. You would not fear dinosaurs that were herbivores because they would not want to eat you.)

Q5. *This answer is based on personal thought. You can choose any answer as long as it is clearly written.*

(For example, you might think that dinosaurs became extinct because meat eating dinosaurs over ruled all of the other dinosaurs, and therefore wiped those ones out. You could then mention the theory of the dinosaurs being wiped out by a meteorite.)

Q6. Brachiosaurus

Q7. The statement that scientists believed the Brachiosaurus to be warm blooded could be disputed, through the use of the word 'believed'. They are not completely sure, and therefore the word believed is used to suggest assumption.

Superhero Showdown

Q1. Persuasive text

Q2. The text is trying to persuade you to attend the Superhero Showdown. It is an invite to an event which uses emotive language to encourage the reader to attend. An advert is used to persuade. It uses rhetorical questions, and stirring language to emphasise the positives of the product or event that is being advertised.

Q3. *This answer is based on personal thought. You can choose any answer so long as you support your answer with evidence from the text*

(For example, you could say that you are persuaded to attend the showdown. The use of fun, superhero characters draws you in immediately. The use of the word 'showdown' suggests a battle, which instantly makes you want to watch. The text and images catch my eye and the use of rhetorical questions makes me want to find out what it's all about. The use of repetition with the 'five Fs' makes it sound more exciting and captivating.)

Q4. Alliteration

Q5. Alliteration is a great way to create rhythm and a pattern in a text. This allows the text to sound more upbeat and exciting. It creates a particular mood and adds emphasis. It evokes sound and entices the audience.

Q6. The use of the phrase "have you ever wondered what it's like to be a superhero?" makes the text more personal. The writer is pulling their readers in, by personalising it to them. The reader will then consider this question, which means the text is thought-provoking and interactive.

Q7. 3 adults = £5.00 x 3 = £15.00

2 children (under the age of 5) = FREE

3 children (over the age of 5) = £2.10 x 3 = £6.30

£15.00 + £6.30 = £21.30

Understanding 'The Green Cross Code'

Q1. You are advised not to cross diagonally as opposed to crossing in a straight line because this would take longer, and therefore would be more hazardous.

Q2. Don't stand behind parked cars and on corners.

Q3. Zebra, puffin, pelican and toucan crossings.

Q4. Instruction

Q5. You are able to tell that the text is based on instructions through the use of a step-by-step guide. The text numbers the key points and advises you how to cross the road safely. In an instruction text, it often uses sub-headings and step-by-step methods to tell someone how to do something in the correct/safest way.

Q6. It is important not to stand too close to the kerb when looking for traffic because if traffic is approaching, you might be caught by a vehicle. This is especially true for cyclists because they ride closer to the kerb.

Q7. Sight

Q8. The definition of a hazard is something that appears to cause danger or a risk to someone or something. For example, children playing with a football on the footpath is a risk to drivers, as they need to be vigilant in case the ball or child come off the path into the road.

Q9. Stand in a place where you are not hidden.

Wearing bright coloured or florescent clothing.

Q10. *This answer is based on personal thought*

(For example, you could have written that 'The Green Cross Code' is so named because a code is something that you need to follow. 'Green Cross' could imply that it is 'good to go'. For example, a green traffic light means 'go', so if you put the words together, it is actually saying wait until it is safe to do so, by following the codes of conduct, and cross the road safely.)

Global Warming

Q1. Based on the passage, the term "fluctuate" is referring to the dramatic changes in the weather.

Q2. Weather conditions may become extremely hot.

Some places may experience torrential rain.

Some places may experience plummeting temperatures.

Q3. Deforestation

Burning fossil fuels

Q4. The author uses the word 'we' to describe us as a society to draw the reader in and make it more effective. The use of the word 'we' makes it more personal, and therefore it addresses the reader directly.

Q5. One fifth

Q6. Global warming is a result of man-made behaviour.	✔
Global warming will see all temperatures rise.	✘
Deforestation plays no role in global warming.	✘
Burning fossil fuels is a contributing factor to global warming.	✔
Moose expel methane which produces carbon dioxide.	✔

Unexplained Object in British Skies

Q1. This is a newspaper article. One way you can tell this is that the writing is formatted into columns, which is how articles are presented in print form. Also, the writing is in a reporting style, and uses quotes and a headline. It is also presented with a picture.

Q2. You can assume that 'Unexplained Object in British Skies' is talking about something unusual and uncommon. The fact that it is 'unexplained' means that it is difficult to determine what it *actually* was, and therefore you can assume it is an article based on alien activity or UFOs.

Q3. Unknown

"The first incident was reported at 08:16am on Wednesday, and the unnamed witness claims to have been "fetching her daily newspaper" when the extraordinary thing happened."

Q4. This article is not completely reliable because it is only based on what was witnessed by three people. The fact that the last sentence states "neither of the witnesses were able to film nor capture the event on camera" demonstrates the fact that there is no proof to suggest that this event *actually* happened.

Q5. 08:16am

Q6. Flat object

Slight yellow tinge

Triangular shaped

Q7. Gliding and hovering

You may have other words which mean the same thing. Check this with a parent or teacher.

Q8. A regular heartbeat

Q9. 2000 miles

Q10. Like a shooting star

The Human Body

Q1. (1) Skull, (2) Collar Bone, (3) Ribs / Rib Cage, (4) Spine, (5) Pelvis, (6) Thigh Bone, (7) Knee cap

Q2. Protecting your body parts

Supporting your body

Lets you move

Q3. Jellyfish

Worm

Q4. Joints are where two bones join together. These joints allow us to bend. Knee caps are a joint because they allow you to bend your leg. They help you to run, walk and sit.

Q5. Our spine is vital in our human body. It allows us to stand up straight and gives us posture. It also protects the spinal nerves in our back.

Q6. Heart and lungs

Q7.

All animals have a skeleton.	✗
Muscles are attached to bones using tendons.	
The lungs are the most important muscle in the body.	
Our bones grow as we grow.	
Horses have a backbone.	
Only one muscle is needed in order to contract.	
Based on the information, an elbow is a bone joint.	

The Water Cycle

Q1. Water vapour

Q2. The word recycled can be defined as reusing material. The water cycle reuses water as it works in an eternal process. From evaporation, to condensation, to precipitation, the water is being transformed into different forms, but is being used again and again.

Q3. Condensation

Q4. Explanation text

This is an explanation text because it is describing and explaining how something works. Texts that describe the life cycle of something are providing an account of how or why something happens in a particular way.

Q5. When water evaporates, it fills the air. This turns into water vapour, and as this water cools down and turns into tiny water droplets, these droplets then form a cloud.

Q6. *All you have to do for this answer is just reword the steps of the water cycle process. Get a parent or teacher to read your response. Remember, make sure it is in your own words.*

Q7. If there was a lack of rainfall, this means part of the water cycle process would become disrupted. If the weather was hot and there weren't many rainy days, then rain would not be falling into the rivers or seas, and therefore water supply would slowly decrease.

HOW ARE YOU GETTING ON?

WRITING A PLAY

WRITING A PLAY

WHAT IS A PLAY?

A play is a form of literature that is written by a **playwright**, which is intended to be **performed** on stage, radio, TV or film.

The layout of a **script** is really important. Apart from looking aesthetically pleasing, it needs to be clear and *look* like a play script.

A PLAY SCRIPT

<u>A script contains TWO main elements in order to convey the style of a play:</u>

Dialogue

- A conversation between characters. In a literary text, the name of the character always appears on the left side of the page, followed by what they say. Each character's dialogue is written on a separate line.

Stage directions

- Instructions for both the actors and director. Usually written in italics or brackets. These instructions tell the actors how to enter the scene, how they should speak or move, and how props need to be used.

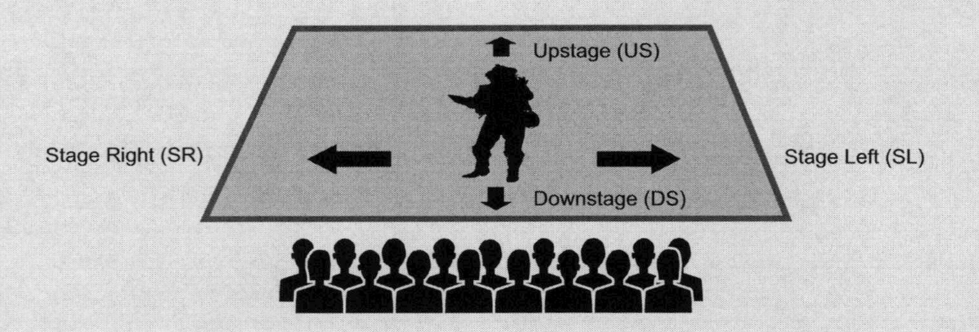

WRITING A PLAY

THE STRUCTURE OF A PLAY

A play is broken up into different **scenes**. These scenes act similarly to chapters in a book.

The scenes also allow for interval (or intermission) so that the audience and actors can have a break during a live performance.

These scenes make up an **act**.

ACT 1	ACT 2	ACT 3	ACT 4
Scene 1	Scene 1	Scene 1	Scene 1
Scene 2	Scene 2	Scene 2	Scene 2
Scene 3	Scene 3	Scene 3	Scene 3
Scene 4	Scene 4	Scene 4	Scene 4

THINGS TO CONSIDER

Although the layout of the play script is important, there are other things that need to be considered:

Plot or narrative

- Every successful play needs a great storyline.

Scenery or mise-en-scène

- Everything you see on the set.

Characters

- This includes the number of characters, appearance, body language how they act.
- **Characterisation** is extremely important when it comes to plays, as the audience need to be able to identify the role of each character. The way a role is characterised is down to the actor. They bring the character to life.

Costumes

- The costumes need to reflect the narrative and time in which the play is set.

WILLIAM SHAKESPEARE

WHO IS WILLIAM SHAKESPEARE?

William Shakespeare is a famous British poet and playwright, and is still considered one of the greatest writers of literary history.

SHAKESPEARE AND HIS WORK

Shakespeare wrote around 40 plays, 154 sonnets and a whole range of other poetry.

Some of his most well-known plays include:

Romeo and Juliet	Macbeth	Julius Caesar
A Midsummer Night's Dream	The Taming of the Shrew	Much Ado About Nothing
King Lear	Hamlet	Othello

The works of Shakespeare are taught in schools as a way of recognising writing that is in an old-fashioned style.

Due to the time in which Shakespeare was writing (over 400 years ago), his writing style is very different to how we read and write today.

Looking at Shakespeare is a great way for children to learn the importance of language in relation to context. The time in which something is written has great bearing on the writing style which is used. Some modern authors use old-fashioned writing techniques to emphasise that their writing is being placed during a different time period.

WILLIAM SHAKESPEARE

TYPES OF SHAKESPEAREAN PLAYS

There are three types of Shakespearean plays:

1. Comedies
2. Tragedies
3. Histories

Comedies

- This is a different type of humour than what we find funny in today's world.
- Most Shakespearean comedies offer dramatic storylines, alongside their underlying humour.
- Most comedies offer a happy ending.

Characteristics = struggle of young love, element of separation, mistaken identities, interwoven plotlines, use of puns and irony and family conflict / tension.

Tragedies

- Tend to be more serious, dramatic and tense.
- Usually involve death of main character/s.

Characteristics = social breakdown, isolation of main characters, ends in death, noble characters who are brought down by their flaws and no escape from the drama.

Histories

- Focus on English monarchs including King John, Richard II, Henry VIII and loads more.
- Use of Elizabethan propaganda.
- Dangers of civil war and conflict.
- Present a particular image of monarchs, although often considered as misrepresentations and inaccurate.

Characteristics = use of English monarchs to centre the storyline, glorify ancestors, depict monarchs in a particular way, and use conflict and tragedy to dramatise the narrative.

WILLIAM SHAKESPEARE

THE USE OF LANGUAGE

Many people struggle to understand the works of Shakespeare, because his writing style and language is extremely different to ours.

The use of old-fashioned language made it difficult for readers to interpret, but these words and phrases were often worked out by understanding the rest of the script.

<u>Example from Macbeth:</u>

MACBETH
To-night we hold a solemn supper sir,
And I'll request your presence.

BANQUO
Let your highnessCommand upon me; to the which my duties
Are with a most indissoluble tie
For ever knit.

MACBETH
Ride you this afternoon?

BANQUO
Ay, my good lord.

Shakespeare also used poetry techniques in his plays. The characters in his plays would sometimes speak in a poetic form, and this allowed the play to gain rhythm and pace in regards to language and dialogue.

Read the text carefully and answer the following questions.

Extract from *Romeo and Juliet* by William Shakespeare.

ACT II **Scene II** *(Capulet's orchard).*

[Juliet appears above at a window]

ROMEO. But soft! what light through yonder window breaks?
It is the east and Juliet is the sun.
Arise, fair sun, and kill the envious moon,
Who is already sick and pale with grief
That thou, her maid, art far more fair than she.
Be not her maid, since she is envious;
Her vestal livery is but sick and green,

And none but fools do wear it. Cast it off!
It is my lady, O, it is my love!
O that she knew she were!
She speaks, yet she says nothing; what of that?
Her eye discourses, I will answer it.
I am too bold: 'tis not to me she speaks.
Two of the fairest stars in all the heaven,
Having some business, do entreat her eyes
To twinkle in their spheres till they return.
What if her eyes were there, they in her head?
The brightness of her cheek would shame those stars,
As daylight doth a lamp. Her eyes in heaven
Would through the airy region stream so bright
That birds would sing and think it were not night.
See how she leans her cheek upon her hand.
O that I were a glove upon that hand,
That I might touch that cheek!

JULIET. Ay me!

ROMEO. She speaks. *(Aside)*
O, speak again, bright angel, for thou art
As glorious to this night, being o'er my head,
As is a winged messenger of heaven
Unto the white-upturned wondering eyes
Of mortals that fall back to gaze on him

Question 1

Where is the scene taking place?

____

Question 2

What act and scene is this extract taken from?

____

Question 3

The first line appears in brackets, and is written in italics. Why are they written this way and what do they show?

____

____

____

Question 4

Which two characters are in this scene?

____________________ and ____________________

Question 5

What does Romeo mean by the term "envious"?

____

Question 6

What do you think Shakespeare is talking about when he uses the term "winged messenger"?

____

Question 7

What is happening in this scene? Tick **one**.

A battle ☐

An argument ☐

A declaration of marriage ☐

A declaration of love ☐

Question 8

Romeo talks about the moon, calling it “sick and pale with grief”. What literary technique is this? Tick **one**.

Alliteration ☐

Analogy ☐

Personification ☐

Metaphor ☐

Question 9

Find a quote which highlights how Romeo compares Juliet to the stars. What does this mean in terms of his feelings for her?

____

____

____

____

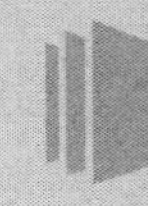

Question 10

Shakespeare contrasts day with night. What do you think this means in terms of Romeo and Juliet's relationship?

Question 11

Romeo is standing in Juliet's garden. What could the garden symbolise in terms of motifs and themes?

Question 12

Why do you think Romeo is talking to Juliet from a distance, as opposed to going up to speak to her?

Read the text carefully and answer the following questions.

Extract from *Macbeth* by William Shakespeare.

ACT II Scene II

Enter ***Macbeth,*** *with bloody daggers*

LADY MACBETH. My husband!

MACBETH. I have done the deed. Didst thou not hear a noise?

LADY MACBETH. I heard the owl scream and the crickets cry. Did not you speak?

MACBETH. When?

LADY MACBETH. Now.

MACBETH. As I descended?

LADY MACBETH. Ay.

MACBETH. Hark! Who lies i' th' second chamber?

LADY MACBETH. Donalbain.

MACBETH. *(looking at his hands)* This is a sorry sight.

LADY MACBETH. A foolish thought, to say a sorry sight.

MACBETH. There's one did laugh in's sleep, and one cried.
"Murder!"
That they did wake each other. I stood and heard them.
But they did say their prayers, and addressed them
Again to sleep.

LADY MACBETH. There are two lodged together.

MACBETH. One cried, "God bless us!" and "Amen" the other,
As they had seen me with these hangman's hands.
List'ning their fear I could not say "Amen,"
When they did say "God bless us!"

LADY MACBETH. Consider it not so deeply.

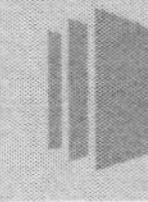

Question 1

What do you think Shakespeare is referring to with the phrase, "I have done the deed"?

____

____

____

____

Question 2

What object does Macbeth enter the scene holding? Circle **one**.

SWORD **GUN** **KNIFE** **DAGGER**

Question 3

When Lady Macbeth says, "Consider it not so deeply", what do you think she is saying? Tick **one**.

Macbeth needs to think about it more. ☐

Donalbain needs to think about what has happened. ☐

Macbeth needs to think about it less. ☐

Lady Macbeth is outraged by what she has seen. ☐

Question 4

What two noises did Lady Macbeth hear?

____________________ and ____________________

Question 5

What two stage directions are written? Quote them exactly from the extract.

1. ______________________________

____

2. ______________________________

____

Question 6

What chamber is mentioned in the extract? Circle **one**.

FIRST **SECOND** **THIRD** **FOURTH** **FIFTH**

Question 7

What adjective is used to describe the voices after "they had seen me with these hangman's hands"?

____

Question 8

The use of the words "hangman's hands" is an example of which literary technique? Tick **one**.

Personification ☐

Alliteration ☐

Simile ☐

Irony ☐

Question 9

What do you think the author means by the phrase “hangman’s hands”?

Question 10

Why do you think Macbeth was unable to say “Amen”? What does this say to the reader about the character of Macbeth?

Question 11

What does the word “descended” mean?

Question 12

The themes of death and violence are emphasised in this extract. What does this suggest about the rest of the narrative?

Read the text carefully and answer the following questions.

Extract from *Blaze and the Crystal Diadem* by How2Become.

ACT I Scene IV

*[Enter **BLAZE** and **Preston**. Blaze is a boy no older than 15 but is known for all manners of trouble. Flickers of yellow, orange and red pour from his hands in anger and frustration. Preston is a sweet, polite boy whose aim is to make the world a safer place].*

BLAZE. Remember me! For I am your own worst enemy. You stand no chance against the Almighty Blaze.

PRESTON. It's not too late Blaze. You can stop all of this now. Don't make it any worse for yourself.

BLAZE. *(Laughs in amusement)* Please! Do you really think you can take me on? Let's take a look shall we – have you seen yourself compared to me?*(Looks Preston up and down and smirks).* All you have is a cape and high-heeled boots. Me... well... you know what I'm capable of.

PRESTON. Ok, you leave me no other choice.

*(Preston whistles. The sounds of a hummingbird. Blaze makes a run for it but is soon stopped in his tracks. Enter **Scarlett**, **Lalita**, **Freddie** and **Anil**. They have Blaze cornered.*

SCARLETT. Give us the diadem! *(Blaze is holding a jewelled, shiny object only fit for Queen. Its powers are way beyond anything that anyone could imagine, and in the wrong hands, the consequences could be catastrophic.)*

FREDDIE. You can't win this, Blaze. You're finished.

BLAZE. You underestimate me Freddie boy.

(In that instant, Blaze's hands begin to lighten up. As he swings his arms in all directions, burning flames rise from the ground).

PRESTON. Everybody, move!

(The inferno surrounded everyone, causing them to back off. With the air filled with flames, it was difficult to see. Preston manages to spot Blaze's cackling face. And with one clap of Blaze's hands, he was gone.)

*[Exit **Blaze**]*

Question 1

What act and scene is the extract from?

____

Question 2

Why do you think the writer has used the name 'Blaze'? Give examples from the extract.

____

____

____

____

Question 3

Why do you think the writer uses the stage direction, "looks Preston up and down and smirks"? What effect does this have on the audience?

____

____

____

____

Question 4

Based on your understanding of the extract, what do you think a diadem is? Give examples from the extract.

____

____

____

____

Question 5

What do the colours in this extract symbolise?

____

____

____

____

Question 6

Why do you think Preston whistles?

____

____

____

____

Question 7

Who does not have an active voice in this extract? Tick **all** that apply.

Preston ☐

Anil ☐

Freddie ☐

Blaze ☐

Scarlett ☐

Lalita ☐

Question 8

Based on the extract, what do you think the aim of this narrative is? Circle **one**.

REVENGE **GOOD VS EVIL** **LOVE** **FRIENDSHIP**

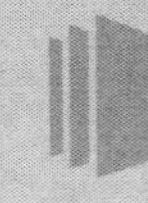

Question 9

Based on your answer to Question 8, explain how you know this. Use at least **two** examples from the text and show how this relates to the aim of the narrative.

Question 10

What does the phrase, "its powers are way beyond anything that anyone could imagine" mean?

Question 11

How does the character of Blaze show that he deems himself superior?

Question 12

Using the extract as a starting point, continue on the script with what you think happens next. Pay attention to spelling, grammar and play techniques.

Read the text carefully and answer the following questions.

Extract from *Maddie and the Stardust* by How2Become.

ACT I Scene I

[In the darkness, a soft voiceover begins].

VOICEOVER. A long, long time ago, in a forest once ruled by a King and Queen, lived their beautiful daughter, Madeline. With hair as golden as the sun, and eyes that mirrored the ocean, Maddie was considered all things beautiful, all things graceful, and all things pure.

Hidden deep in the forest lived a wicked old lady. Over 500 years old, the woman continued to exist by feasting off the blood of the young. The old lady was never recognised though, for she continued to get younger after every meal.

[Down by the river, sparkling bright like a crystal diamond, Maddie sat looking into the deep, blue water. Her tears touched the surface water. A flash of lightening flickered through the ripples, and caught Maddie's attention].

SPIRIT. Dear child, do not cry. For it is I...

[Maddie looked into the water and was perplexed to find a reflection of someone in the water. She looked behind her to see if anyone was there, no one].

Your presence in this forest is so pure. A spell that was cast on you, for there is no cure. For you will die if blood is taken, heaven forsaken. You know of the evil and of the dark, as old and as ragged as a dying tree's bark. Here is some stardust, of which the wicked will lust. Its wonders are of power, for every waking hour. Make a wish and wait for light, for it will guide you even in the darkest of nights.

MADDIE. Whaa...? Who.... Are you?

SPIRIT. Oh child, do not worry, you won't be sorry. Remember what I told you, your purity and love and grace can be used to make wishes come true.

[The reflection in the water begins to fade and the ripples in the water gets faster].

Question 1

What type of narrative is this extract taken from? Circle **one**.

ROMANCE **HORROR** **MUSICAL** **FAIRYTALE**

How do you know?

Question 2

Why do you think the extract begins with a voiceover? What effect would this have on an audience?

Question 3

Where is the scene set? Describe the scene.

Question 4

How does the old lady continue to survive?

____

____

____

____

Question 5

What role do you think the old lady plays in this story? Using examples from the extract, explain why you think this.

____

____

____

____

Question 6

In the extract, the writer uses the word "perplexed". Out of the following, which best describes the meaning of this word? Tick **one**.

Completely overwhelmed ☐

Caught off guard ☐

Completely frightened ☐

Completely baffled ☐

Showed no interest ☐

Question 7

Explain why you think the play script has used ellipses in the sentence "Whaa...? Who... are you?"

Question 8

The writer uses a simile in this extract. Write this simile and explain why it's been used.

Question 9

The extract begins with a conversation between Maddie and a Spirit. Why do you think the writer has used a Spirit? What importance do you think it will have on the rest of the story?

Question 10

What can you assume from the phrase “in a forest once ruled by a King and Queen”?

Question 11

The Spirit hands Maddie stardust. What do you suppose the Spirit wants Maddie to do with it?

Question 12

Describe the way the Spirit talks. How does this change the rhythm of the play? How do you think the audience will respond to this characterisation?

ANSWERS TO UNDERSTANDING POETRY

Romeo and Juliet

Q1. Capulet's Orchard.

Q2. Act II Scene II

Q3. The first line is written in italics and in brackets because this indicates stage directions. In plays, there are dialogue and stage directions. The stage directions show how the characters move, act or behave and they highlight key things regarding the scene.

Q4. Romeo and Juliet

Q5. The term "envious" means jealous.

Q6. The term "winged messenger" suggest angel-like features. Angels send messages down from heaven, and this is how Romeo sees Juliet, standing above him in the window.

Q7. A declaration of love.

Q8. Personification

Q9. "Two of the fairest stars in all the heaven / Having some business do entreat her eyes". This suggests that Romeo sees Juliet as being as bright and beautiful as the stars above. It shows Romeo's love for Juliet by comparing her to something idyllic and beautiful.

Q10. Shakespeare compares day and night in this scene in order to demonstrate the good and bad in Romeo and Juliet's lives. It emphasises opposing forces in their relationship. This suggests that Romeo and Juliet's relationship could be seen as a struggle or conflict.

Q11. The garden could symbolise freedom, peace and love. Gardens are a way of creating a safe enclosure. It could also represent innocence and purity.

Q12. Romeo might be talking to Juliet from below her window because he is not meant to be talking to her. He must remain hidden, which is why he is unable to simply knock on the door. Also, it shows the declaration of love between two characters. Romeo is pouring his heart out to the woman he loves and therefore he has put himself in a vulnerable position, hence why he is positioned lower.

Macbeth

Q1. Murder

Q2. Dagger

Q3. Macbeth needs to think about it less.

Q4. Owl scream and crickets cry

Q5. *Enter* ***Macbeth****, with bloody daggers* and *(looking at his hands)*

Q6. Second

Q7. Cried

Q8. Alliteration

Q9. The author uses the words "hangman's hands" to suggest that Macbeth's hands are bloody, and therefore he has committed a crime.

Q10. Macbeth might not have been able to say "Amen" because he didn't want to wake them up. Also, he might not have been able to say it because he felt ashamed before God.

Q11. The word "descended" means move or fall downwards.

Q12. The themes of death and violence are highlighted in this extract. This suggests that Macbeth is a strong, masculine character who uses violence as a way of getting what he wants and showing who is in power. The image of Macbeth's bloody hands and carrying a dagger suggests his violent nature, as well as the lasting consequences of such actions. Therefore, it is possible to say that the narrative of the play is centred on these key ideas and themes.

Blaze and the Crystal Diadem

Q1. Act I Scene IV

Q2. The writer has used the name Blaze because it highlights his superpower. Blaze is able to fire flames from his hands, which is indicated by the yellows, oranges and reds that pour from his hands. At the end of the extract, "Blaze's hands begin to lighten up. As he swings his arms in all directions, burning flames rise from the ground".

Q3. The writer uses the stage direction "looks Preston up and down and smirks" to highlight how Blaze is mocking Preston. By looking someone up and down you are considering everything about them, yet the fact that he smirks, suggests that he is not impressed.

Q4. From the extract, the diadem is a crown or tiara. The fact that the writer states "a jewelled, shiny object only fit for a Queen", suggests that it is a crown.

Q5. The colours red, orange and yellow indicate an inferno, and flames/fire. This suggests that there is conflict in the narrative. It suggests anger, pain or even death. Although flames could symbolise love and passion, the context of the passage suggests that the narrative is based on conflict.

Q6. Preston whistles because this is his way of calling for his other friends. It is like a birdcall and allows the others to know that they are needed.

Q7. Anil, Lalita

Q8. Good vs evil

Q9. The extract is based on good vs evil because Preston and his friends are trying to stop Blaze from stealing the diadem. This clearly shows the relationship between good behaviour vs unacceptable behaviour. Based on the extract, we can assume that Preston and his friends are superheroes and Blaze is a supervillain.

Q10. The phrase "its powers are way beyond anyone could imagine" means that nobody is fully aware of just how powerful the diadem is. Therefore, if the diadem is in the wrong hands it could have severe consequences.

Q11. Blaze deems himself superior through his language. Blaze states "have you seen yourself compared to me? All you have is a cape and high-heeled boots. Me…well…you know what I'm capable of". This suggests that Blaze is mocking Preston and therefore thinks he is better and stronger.

Q12. **You need to continue on with the extract. This can be anything. Make sure that you use the names given, provide dialogue and give appropriate stage directions. Have a teacher or parent look over this for you.*

*In your real test, you will be awarded extra marks for use of language and correct punctuation and spelling.**

Maddie and the Stardust

Q1. Fairy tale.

You know that this extract is taken from a fairy tale narrative, because most fairy tales use a voiceover to begin the story. Also, most narratives begin with 'once upon a time' or 'a long, long time ago'. Finally, the fact that there is a King, Queen, a wicked lady, and a spirit who provides magic stardust all suggest that it's based on a fairy tale.

Q2. The extract begins with a voiceover because it is setting up the scene. A voiceover is used to tell the story whilst it is happening, in order for the audience to gain more background into the narrative. This allows the audience to follow the storyline as well as relate to the characters.

Q3. The scene is set in a forest. A river passes through the forest which is "sparkling bright like a crystal diamond".

Q4. The old lady continues to survive by feasting off the blood of young people.

Q5. The old lady is going to be the villain of this fairy tale. Every fairy tale has a villain, and the fact that the old lady feasts on the blood of young people suggests that Maddie is in danger. Therefore, Maddie will need to fight against her and defeat the evil woman.

Q6. Completely baffled.

Q7. The use of ellipses in the sentence "Whaa...? Who...are you?" suggests that Maddie is confused and maybe a little frightened. Ellipses are used to indicate a pause. This pause in Maddie's dialogue suggests that she is "perplexed" and uncertain about what is happening.

Q8. "With hair as golden as the sun". This allows the audience to visualise Maddie in more detail. The fact that her hair is golden means that she must have light, blonde hair. The audience are given some characteristics of what the protagonist looks like.

Q9. The fact the extract begins with a conversation between Maddie and a Spirit, suggests that Maddie might be lonely and in need of comfort. It could also suggest that she needs guidance. Not only that, but it also draws on elements of fantasy and imagination. This could be important to the rest of the story because the Spirit acts as a guide for what Maddie has to do. The Spirit allows Maddie to defeat evil.

Q10. The phrase "in a forest once ruled by a King and Queen" suggests that the forest is no longer run by the King and Queen. You could infer that they died, and therefore Maddie has been left on her own.

Q11. The Spirit hands Maddie stardust in order to help her defeat the evil old lady. The magic stardust will allow Maddie's wishes to be granted, which should be used only for good, love and purity.

Q12. The way in which the Spirit speaks to Maddie is poetic. It rhymes and therefore adds musicality to the play. This allows the character of the Spirit to be instantly recognisable by the audience. It also creates a positive beat for the audience to follow.

HOW ARE YOU GETTING ON?

NEED A LITTLE EXTRA HELP WITH KEY STAGE 2 (KS2) ENGLISH?

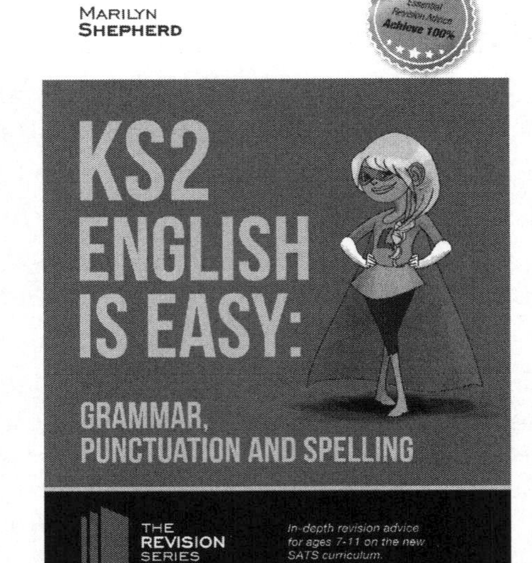

How2Become have created two other FANTASTIC guides to help you and your child prepare for their Key Stage Two (KS2) English SATs.

These exciting guides are filled with fun and interesting facts for your child to engage with to ensure that their revision is fun, and their learning is improved! Invest in your child's future today!

FOR MORE INFORMATION ON OUR KEY STAGE 2 (KS2) GUIDES, PLEASE CHECK OUT THE FOLLOWING:

WWW.HOW2BECOME.COM